The Joy of Talk

KIT FRASER

QUARTET BOOKS

First published in 2010 by
Quartet Books Limited
A member of the Namara Group
27 Goodge Street, London WIT 2LD

A catalogue record for this book
is available from the British Library

ISBN   978 0 7043 7195 8

Typeset by Antony Gray
Printed and bound in Great Britain by
T J International Ltd, Padstow, Cornwall

CONTENTS

INTRODUCTION

Conversation is an art. Not everyone is born with the talent, but our use and enjoyment of words has a huge impact on our lives. Work, friendships, love, fun and power all hinge on an ability to communicate. Whether it's a dinner party or a train journey, conversation matters. Through words we can overcome our insecurities (at least for the duration of the exchange) and make communion with our fellow man.

I am not a natural talker. I come from a silent family in a silent county. My three brothers and I were brought up in Suffolk, a notoriously taciturn county. 'There is one thing about Suffolk folk and that is they find talk terribly difficult,' says a character in the Sixties documentary *Akenfield*.

We four boys spent our happy country childhood *doing things*, not talking. We obsessed about marbles, conkers, ping pong, bows and arrows, bicycles, Waddington games and stamps. All these activities required single-minded concentration, even stamp collecting. I would have done anything for a Cape of Good Hope triangle but my brother Rory got there before me. Talk is just distraction. You don't talk when you are aiming a marble or an arrow or a conker. Deep philately covetousness is silent.

Our parents were themselves brought up to be seen and not heard, so that experience informed their style of parenthood. We were certainly not encouraged to speak in front of adults. When we were sent to boarding school it came as no surprise to us that talking after lights out in the dormitory was a beating offence. My younger brother Anselm used to come home from public school in the holidays and perfect an attitude which he called 'bonse sitting'. This involved sitting down for long stretches of time saying, doing and thinking … absolutely nothing.

Our family has a history of silence. My great-great-grandfather on my mother's side was James Grant, the Victorian explorer who with John Hanning Speke won the race to find the source of the Nile. My great-great-grandfather might not have talked the talk, but he certainly knew how to walk the walk. He was famously laconic with the result that he was one of the very few members of a Victorian expedition who did not argue with everybody else on it. I imagine Grant being interviewed by a reporter on the event of his triumphant return to Britain after his successful trip up the Nile:

> 'Is it true, Mr Grant, that you and your colleague, Mr Speke, have beaten all and sundry from all other nations in the world and won for Britain, her People and her Queen the race in the heart of that dark and dangerous continent of Africa to the source of the Great Nile Herself?'
>
> 'Yes.'
>
> 'And tell me, Mr Grant, was there any moment you thought of giving up in those long weary months of trudging through thickest Africa jungle surrounded by all manner of black heathen savagery, wracked by fatigue, daunted by every conceivable obstacle, beset by danger and plagued by malaria, dysentery and dihatsu – that particularly horrible virus carried on the wing of the Tse Tse fly?'
>
> 'No.'

My grandfather on my father's side was well known for not talking during the day, which he would spend with his gamekeeper. Together they would roam the straths, moors, glens and rivers of the East Highlands surprising bird, beast and fish with their guile, their stealth and yes, their total lack of conversation. The first thing the prey would hear would be the crack of gunfire a moment before their death. He even insisted on silence when fishing, so fish must have ears too.

He would barely say a word through dinner in the evening either but afterwards, with the last plate cleared away and a whisky in his hand, he would finally start to talk. I think it was only after he had percolated his experiences of the day that he thought it was worth making comment. He was an old fashioned countryman.

The point I am making is that by nature and nurture I am one of the silent majority and it has not served me well: I cannot help but notice that it is the talkers who get the good jobs and the pretty girls.

This book is the product of a life long battle to beat my DNA, improve my IQ and acquire what P. G. Wodehouse would have called the 'gift of the gab'.

CHAPTER ONE

Words

1 WORDS ARE THE POINT OF MAN

'In the beginning was the word … ' These are the first six words of *St John's Gospel.* That's his opener. The word preceded man. And then the word became flesh.

So when man finally arrives on the scene, what is he but a vehicle for words? Whether we take the bible literally or not, St John was certainly right about one thing: human beings are conduits for language. Be it orally or through writing, we all perform this function. According to the Bible it is the most significant or sacred thing we do. It is the point of life. It precedes life.

Arguably, the trouble began when man decided he wanted someone to laugh at his jokes. Words weren't much fun when they existed in a vacuum, so God relented and created Eve, who – let's face it – was trouble from the start. Within the next few days everyone in Eden had realised the staggering power of language – to cajole, learn, please and dominate. Words may be sacred, but they're also more powerful than we give them credit for. It is crucial to understand the huge impact words have on our lives.

2 WORDS ENABLE PROGRESS

I like St John's deference for the word as the source of existence, but let's look at the atheist version of things as well. In the beginning was the void. Then out of nowhere with one hell of an explosion, came the universe, which consists of three component parts: matter, energy and information. We have developed from the ape using our ability to process and communicate information, initially by grunts and groans and eventually with language. As our language became more sophisticated, so did our understanding of matter and energy. This translated into increasingly spectacular inventions until in the end, with the advent of the science of genetics, we appear to be imitating God Himself.

A thought can precede a word, but without a word you cannot communicate to another thinker. Man's progress from ape to Einstein started with the spoken word, was accelerated by the written and printed word, and now is whizzing faster than ever before through the Internet. It is the word that has given us power over matter and energy.

3 A WORD IS A NOISE

What is a word? Words are symbols of symbols. They are thus twice removed from reality. Take a car for example. The reality of a car is what it personally means to you. It might mean sitting in a confined space listening to a prat on the radio, or the smell of engine oil. The second remove is the actuality of the car as a concept. Then finally you have the word 'car', which is a sound. I know philosophy of language is an infinite academic discipline that keeps our finest and most erudite academics in a lifelong agony of contemplation, but we have got to get on …

4 WORD-MAKING IS MAN'S PRIMARY INSTINCT

Words are the noises we make to one another in order to communicate our experience of reality. I would argue it is a primary instinct in man. Scotland's first great novelist, Robert Louis Stevenson wrote: 'The first duty of a man is to speak: that is his chief business in the world, and talk which is the harmonious speech of two or more, is by far the most accessible of our pleasures.' The poet, Czeslaw Milosz goes even further when he says: 'What is pronounced strengthens itself. What is not pronounced tends to non-existence.' It is almost as if he is saying that words have the power to bring things into being, which they do in the sense that they draw our attention to particular aspects of reality.

'If you can't give something a name, it doesn't belong to you,' writes American playwright Arthur Miller. 'If you look at a flower and you don't know what it is and you don't know the name of that flower, its different than when you look at it and say: "Oh that's a daisy or a pansy." You get closer to it because you can name it. If you meet somebody and you're just chatting and you don't know their name, it's different than when you do.'

5   A WORD IMPARTS FEELING

Think of words like 'sorry', 'thank you' and 'I love you'. Think of the huge effect such words can have on people. Just to say the word 'sorry' can bridge a hitherto unbridgeable gap. It is a word that never fails to bring the prick of tears to my eyes. 'Home' and 'mother' are other huge words.

Neurologists from the universities of London, Birmingham and Warwick have shown that Agatha Christie peppers her prose with words and phrases that act as a trigger to raise levels of serotonin and endorphins, the chemical messengers in the brain that induce pleasure and satisfaction. These are words such as 'she', 'yes', 'girl', 'kind', 'smiled' and 'suddenly'.

There is such a thing as a 'feel' for words. We all have it to a lesser or greater degree. Flip through a dictionary and, if you make yourself aware of it, you will notice yourself having a pronounced reaction to all sorts of nouns, adjectives and verbs. For example I like the words 'luscious' and 'disgusting', but dislike the word 'naff' and can't stand the word 'robust'. I would never use the word 'scam'. I prefer 'wheeze'.

Each word has its payload of emotion and meaning. The sexiest word in the English language is 'tits'. The most important word is 'although'. The conjunction 'although' is integral. At the heart of decision-making is an essential duality. Listen to truly educated people passing judgment. Their opinions invariably hinge on 'although' or its variations. This is a sign of civilisation.

6   A WORD IS A LABEL

Most people use words as labels to save themselves from having to think about an issue. We tend to accept labels that are in common currency or have been handed down to us by recognised experts. However the originators of such labels have often designed them for a particular purpose, usually to manipulate our experience of reality. A classic example is the phrase: 'binge drinking', used by the government and the NHS in an effort to combat the popular notion that a huge consumption of alcohol is a sign of manhood. Children 'binge'. It's a word straight out of Enid Blyton.

The comparatively small town of Inverness, with a population of just 60,000, was rechristened a 'city' in 2003. This simple four-letter word has had a huge impact on our little Northern conurbation. It has actually swayed investment decisions in favour of the place, exaggerating a property and business boom we have recently been enjoying. Public spending has had to reflect our improved status and letters pour into the local newspaper insisting on higher standards of this and that, now that we are a city.

And didn't you just love the revolution in higher education that happened under Tony Blair, when he tripled the number of universities in England simply by renaming scores of polytechnics? The technical colleges all had their nameplates changed and everybody felt much better, at least for a while.

Of course the British are masters at this. Our whole social system is based on it. Little four and six letter words like 'duke', 'lord', 'earl', 'baron', 'dame' and 'knight' are dangled as carrots for high achievement and they don't cost the government a penny. People lower down the pecking order are happy to be rewarded with just a few letters, like OBE or MBE.

7 A WORD IS A GRENADE

A scary characteristic of words is that they can change our perception. The job of a political spin-doctor is to manipulate mass opinion using crafty language. The prime minister is to be described as 'determined' rather than 'stubborn', 'flexible' rather than 'irresolute', and 'bold' rather than 'foolhardy'. Most rows between people do not concern the facts of a case, but their interpretation. Words are so dangerous that one misplaced word can cause an international incident in diplomatic circles, or cause chaos in the stock market. One word, 'yes', put an end to my marriage. It was also the word that brought it into being in the first place.

CHAPTER TWO

Power

1 POWER COMES FROM THE LIPS OF MAN

Power is knowing what to say next. You can be sitting next to a billionaire or a film actress and if you know what to say and they are at a loss for words, in that encounter you are the more powerful. Anything is obtainable, whether it is a promotion or the woman of your dreams, if you have a command of language. 'I have come into my strength / And words obey my call,' boasts the poet Yeats in his poem *Words*.

If you can talk and listen well, the world is your oyster. You can do what you want and enjoy yourself all the time, with anybody you choose. It is the proof of free will. It is the secret of enjoyment.

2 ENGLISH IS A MAGIC MIX

The Romans ruled the known world because they had developed a language of control. Nobody likes to be told what to do. Having said that, the most effective way of issuing instructions without causing offence is to use neutral words, ones without emotional association, so that they do not provoke any emotional reaction. The Romans came up with the perfect language for the job: Latin. You could use it in command without offending anybody because it was made up of words without feeling.

In Malcolm Bradbury's *The History Man*, a character named Howard describes the effect of his father's death. 'One inevitably recognises the removal of the psychic focus of paternalist constraint,' Howard explains in words that are almost entirely of Latin derivation. He continues: 'Of course, I cared for him a lot'. When

Howard articulates sentiment, he reverts to Anglo-Saxon: simpler, plainer, more powerful words.

So the Romans did not have to rely on fear to get their soldiers and civil servants to obey them. They could develop a chain of command where you obeyed your superior without resentment. Morale is a massive positive stimulant to the successful workings of any organisation. Football matches are won on the back of it. The other advantage of using a mechanical language like Latin is that no emotion meant no obfuscation. To this day all language employed by lawyers in a court of law are culled from Latin.

The combination of Anglo-Saxon and Latin has made English the language of choice for the world. The English language can articulate the head and the heart.

3   CONVERSATION BESTOWS CHARISMA

Look at how charisma attaches itself to certain people at a party. You can generate a huge amount of power by successful connection with another person. You can also generate it on your own, of course. That is the point of prayer, education, sport and work. Prayer gives you grace, education develops your intelligence, sport makes you fit and work earns you self-respect. Yet you can be the strongest, holiest, richest, brainiest person in the world; if you can't truly express yourself life will be merely a duty.

'At our roots of being lies not the greed for property or money but the desire, large as a universe, to express ourselves freely and to the utmost limits of our individual capabilities,' writes Constantine Fitzgibbon in her *The Life of Dylan Thomas*. 'When a real self finds language and manages to speak it is surely a dazzling event,' agrees Ted Hughes. And the spiritual world concurs with the literary world. As John O'Donohue writes in the spiritual work *Anam Cara*: 'Each of us needs to learn the unique language of our soul.'

As I write, there is currently widespread media coverage of Alain de Botton's book about the Roman philosopher Epicurus, who knew that money and power did not buy you happiness. Happiness, he observed, came from friendship, thought and freedom. What Epicurus doesn't take into account is the complicated nature of power. Charisma, in my opinion, is the outward sign of an inner power. Charisma will give you the friends that Epicurus so rightly identifies as the source of happiness.

Thought without words is the curse of ignorance. Words are what unlock thoughts and give you the freedom to make friends with anybody you want.

4   FREEDOM COMES FROM SELF DISCIPLINE

Freedom is the third of Epicurus' goals. Self-education is a private, internal battle, mortal combat with mental incompetence. If you win, you are free. Before winning, you have hope. If you lose by giving up, you become the slave of your body – not a pretty sight in old age.

Freedom is the prize being offered by this book. What is freedom and what does it feel like? Let me tell you a story about a rabbit. Have you ever watched a tame rabbit? It's a totally different colour to a wild rabbit. Instead of being a colour that blends in with nature, it sticks out a mile – black with white socks. A tame rabbit is like a man in black tie and tails going for a country walk.

We have got a pet rabbit for our kids. Its world is a hutch. It can stay stock still for hours, as if watching television. Then it jumps down from its specially constructed platform (as if going for a cup of tea during the adverts) and takes a sip of water from the bowl laid out for it. Then it might clean itself. Then another long period of stillness.

I once put our rabbit out in the middle of a field, just for the hell of it. It was unaware that it could move more than a couple of paces. It just stayed as still as it normally does when watching telly. It nibbled away at the grass. Then it moved on a bit, to another area close by. Then it moved once more. Then suddenly, it scampered eight yards or so and I only just managed to grab it before it took off forever. I felt the rabbit's body through the fur. It was trembling all over with excitement, as if it could leap out of my arms any moment. For the first time of the many times I had lifted it, it seemed to have a will of its own.

The paradox of freedom is that it does not come out of chaos. You only have to see the aftermath of revolution to realise that. Freedom comes from total control. An artist only gains freedom of artistic expression after years of self-discipline and a rigorous adherence to the truth. It is the same with words. Freedom was the hippies' mantra but their chronic self-indulgence dissipated their energies and slackened their use of language, making them incapable of liberating themselves let alone the world around them. 'I really dig it man. It's like totally cool. I'm gonna crash' is not the kind of talk to energise a person.

What I advocate in this book is the need to gain command of language in order to make a servant of your mind. Then you are free to do and say what you want. That is power and, incidentally, it is also pleasure. Pleasure is a product of control. If you control a thing – whether it is a motorbike, a white water raft, or a conversation – it gives you pleasure, which is why people do it. Control freaks are not just frightened people; they are also striving for pleasure. Friendship, on the other hand, is the sharing of pleasure. It is an exchange of control. I control you, you control me.

5 BEING GOOD IS NOT ENOUGH

With all this emphasis on power, I am aware of the need, having acquired it, to put it to good use. But that is not the concern of this book. Read *The New Testament* if you want to know what to do with personal power once you've got it. My point is that virtue without power is what you see at Bring and Buy sales at village church fetes. That is not what we're striving for with this book.

Goodness has its limitations. You can be as good as gold, nice as ninepence and as boring as fuck. My uncle once famously said to me: 'There goes a typical Basingstoke man – very nice with nothing to say for himself.'

I berate my schoolgirl daughter, Angie for going out with a guy who constantly two-times her. If I point out a 'nice' guy and ask her why she couldn't go out with him, my daughter says: 'Because he looks dull, Dad.'

Nice is often just not having the courage to be yourself. At least bad is honest. And the good, macho thing about being bad is that bad boys genuinely don't care what other people think. Girls like that. All the rest of us are controlled by other peoples' good opinion.

So beware nice people because you don't know who they are. It is very difficult to tell the difference between people who are good through choice and those who follow the need to conform to social convention. My tip is to look for the fun factor. If they are fun, then the goodness is genuine. Religious fanatics are not exactly fun and that's why for all their prayer, they tend not to be good.

You can only afford to be affectionate and considerate and amused and interested – what I call the *real* virtues – when you feel good about yourself in the company of others. It is a luxury beyond your reach if you are struggling to keep your conversational head above water or, worse still, if you are feeling what I call the *Ins* of thought: inadequate, inarticulate, insecure and incompetent.

Somebody who is drowning thinks only of himself. You can rescue other people and give then a good time only if you are the man in the powerboat. So the Christian virtues are power dependent. The two sources of power that govern goodness are love and knowledge. And we are aware that real knowledge does not mean knowing a million facts like the name of the capital of Peru. It means knowing how to talk to all varieties of human being.

'To be strong is to be happy and expressing our feelings makes us strong and therefore happy,' said Yeats the painter to his son Yeats the poet. Obviously the son took this parental advice to heart because he very successfully devoted the rest of his life to words. It brought him the homage of his beloved country and global fame and any woman he wanted apart from the one he loved. Dammit!

Expressing yourself involves two activities: the ability to be yourself and the ability to use language appropriate to yourself. Where a lot of people go wrong is in conforming to a generalised way of talking in order to articulate a version of themselves that they imagine to be attractive to a perceived audience. Instead of being themselves, a lot of people project an image of themselves.

6   TO BE OR TO ACT

'To be or not to be / That is the question,' and most people in this modern world aren't. By 'aren't', I mean that they are not themselves. The question is not just whether Hamlet should kill himself or not, but whether he should *be* himself or not. Perhaps he should project an acceptable version of himself to fit in with society, or perhaps he should not.

A lot of people are not fully themselves today because they are divorced from their culture. Ex-public schoolboys sent away to boarding school at the tender age of seven, eight or nine lose cultural attachment to their home town or county. Other people lose that connection through overexposure to television, videos and the Internet.

Culture comes from the generational interaction between man and place as expressed in language. A public schoolboy loses his local accent and dialect and with it a very important cultural energy source called the particularity of home. His culture is merely national. So he operates at half power. Over-modernised people can be equally disempowered for reasons of dilution and inflation.

The result of this cultural castration is to make people act as if they had connection and so you get people behaving like actors or salesmen. They project an inflated and supposedly attractive version of themselves because they have lost themselves. My wife Sarah used to describe the experience of talking to ex-public schoolboys as peering into an abyss, into a void of silence. She said she would get a sense of psychic vertigo.

People who are cut off from their culture tend to treat conversation as a performance. For these people cultural disconnection can only be compensated for by acquiring immense verbal and social expertise. Not a bad strategy.

7   LIFE IS ALSO A PERFORMANCE

The outside is as important as the inside. If you have a reduced inside, a great way of enlarging it is by improving your outside.

It is a genuine alternative to psychotherapy, which works the other way around. And it has the advantage of being a lot more amusing even if you don't succeed because, of course, neither method can guarantee personal salvation. Shakespeare says life is a performance. 'All the world's a stage,' he famously decreed. Performance does not have to be hollow. It should be an outward manifestation of an inner grace.

Nobody ever told me when I left school with a fist full of O and A levels that it is not what you know, or even who you know, that matters in the outside world. You are judged on only one thing: how you speak. Your accent, quantity, quality, content, style, tone, speed and manner. Yes, behind your back you are judged on how you behave, but you can't see behind your back so what the hell does that matter. Shakespeare was right. Put on a good show because the quality of your life depends on it.

8   WORDS WOO WOMEN

Words can get you what you want. Classically men fall in love through their eyes and women through their ears. You have to woo a woman (I call it striptease, you tease them and then they strip). Words can woo men, too, but let's talk about women for a moment. If you can talk well, you can have any woman you want. You do not need to be well off or good looking to get the woman of your dreams. You just have to talk her down from her tree of indifference.

'He had always wanted girls to flirt and frolic with him as they did with boys much less handsome and less endowed with this world's goods than he. But on the few occasions when this had happened he could never think of anything to say and he suffered agonies of embarrassment at his dumbness. Then he lay awake at night thinking of all the gallantries he might have employed.' This is Margaret Mitchell writing about Charles Hamilton in *Gone with the Wind.*

9   THE FIVE METHODS OF TALK

Talk can be highly effective in getting the better of somebody in a discussion – whether with a member of the opposite sex or a business acquaintance – without being the slightest bit logical or even reasonable. The same applies to political speeches where you are trying to put one over the general public. There are five methods: speed, emotion, volume, quantity and repetition. By employing all five methods of delivery, Hitler persuaded an innately rational nation to communally take leave of its senses. He gave lengthy, repetitive, emotional tirades at full speed and at full volume. The logic was ludicrous, the arguments spurious; but they swallowed it hook, line and stinker. Hitler was the ultimate talk professional: such a formidable windbag that he suffered chronic flatulence. He had to take sixteen anti-flatulence pills a day.

Let's start with repetition. The whole of advertising, the ultimate persuader, is based on that simple device. Say the same thing enough times and amazingly people start to believe you.

Education is done through repetition. It is how we get from our short term to our long-term memory. Most people's listening skills are so weak that if you don't repeat yourself they won't even hear you. The self help book *Persuasion* by James Borg, about how to be an effective communicator in the work place, advises a manager to explain what he is planning to say, then actually say it, and then say what he has just said.

Repetition makes available to its practitioner the power of recognition. It is only when you hear a thing a second time that you can say: 'I remember that'. It is only when you see a face a second time that you can have the pleasure of saying to yourself: 'I recognise that.' Repetition is one of man's primary learning tools.

Next we have speed. Most people don't really think. Their interests lie elsewhere. They seek to articulate the norm, the consensus of agreement, which they do fluently and at speed. Suspect anybody whose opinion is delivered at the pace of a salesman.

My cousin, Archie, a top city commercial lawyer, told me a story about the premature triumph of speed. He said that people associate intelligence with speed and that the best City lawyers definitely tend to be quicker than their provincial counterparts. One time he was sent by his London company to Coventry to present a case to a number of Coventry solicitors. He made a brilliant, articulate and fluent presentation to the country lawyers and returned to London without one objection having been raised. However, over the next few days all the conceivable and pertinent objections to his case that could have been made started coming through by e-mail, letter, fax and phone.

There was nothing dim about Ted Hughes, arguably Britain's greatest nature poet of all time, in my opinion beating Wordsworth by a short head. Yet as a working class Yorkshire lad at university, he felt intimidated by the swift verbal facility of the public school element that dominated postwar Oxbridge. 'Hughes had never been at ease among a Cambridge set whose background and social skills gave them a different speed of conversation,' writes his biographer, Elaine Feinstein.

The greatest and most recent practitioner of the art of persuasion by emotional connection must surely be the great emoter himself, former US president Bill Clinton. Despite persistent financial and sexual scandal dogging his every step during his Presidential campaign, Bill Clinton beat the Republican candidate Bob Dole. They shared the male vote almost equally. However, Clinton got 54 per cent of women's votes to Dole's 38 per cent. The third candidate got the rest. Clinton did not win the election through force of argument, but by seduction.

The other element of talk that has nothing to do with quality of thought and yet can give you power over other people is verbal quantity. I call practitioners of this gross art 'Talk Tyrants'. They can quite simply talk you into submission. I see many a woman rule a house by her sheer verbosity. Women do have an edge over men in this department. Their daily average is apparently seven thousand words, while your standard man only utters two thousand.

I have seen 'Talk Tyrants', either at work or in the social field, monopolise the conversation to such an extent that other people are drummed into silence. Faced with this barrage, your mind goes numb. In severe cases it can actually give you a headache. What I do for relief when trapped by a merciless monologist, if social etiquette forbids me to actually leave the room, is get up and open a window.

Volume works too. You only have to see how people react to a microphone. It bestows instant power on the person who gets it, immediately relegating other people to a subservient position. Every stand-up comic has an automatic advantage over a heckler by virtue of the microphone in his hand. Similarly a man with a naturally deep voice has a head-start over somebody with a thin reedy one, irrespective of whatever they are saying.

When we get angry we shout and it is frightening for the person on the receiving end of our rant, even though what we are saying might be the arse end of nonsense. Hitler was a great shouter. He cowed a nation with the magnified volume of his self-righteousness.

A thunderous voice can be persuasive, but at the very least it's quite useful. Increasingly in this day and age, what with televisions and radios and booming music systems, we need to shout just to be heard.

10 THINK OR DROWN

Silence is a casualty of the modern age, which is a shame. Original thought thrives in silence, and it is hard to overestimate the importance of thinking for yourself. Somebody who thinks for himself believes in change and growth, because he will have experienced that phenomenon daily. A free thinker does not believe in fixed certainties and does not subscribe to the tyranny of the normal or what other people consider sensible. Nothing sillier than the world being round to a man from the Middle Ages.

If you don't think for yourself, you will lead the rest of your life at the beck and call of your neighbours, trying to live by their rules, playing their unchanging game. Why not change the game and play by invented rules? If you do not believe in change, by definition you are condemning yourself to a life of endless repetition subject to the law of ever diminishing returns. My wife Sarah observes that most marriages fail because men remain adolescent at heart (no change there), sex degenerates into a sort of sibling affection and people do not believe in growth. They might say they do, but they don't.

So to recap for a moment. Power comes out of the mouth in the form of words. Talk can get you whatever you want, even if you lack intellectual prowess, but if you eschew convention and learn to think for yourself then you can actually change, fundamentally, for the better. Articulation aids thought.

What comes first, the chicken or the egg? Thought or words? The philosopher Wittgenstein came up with the revolutionary concept that we are totally restricted in our thinking by the way that we talk, which in turn is bound by our culture so that, for example, a modern urban middle class agnostic Englishman inevitable thinks totally differently to a female Nigerian villager whose primary concern is food. 'The limits of my language means the limits of my world,' is Wittgenstein's famous dictum. How you talk is who you are and to a large extent it determines how you think.

I can give you one piece of cast-iron evidence. At Bristol University I read politics and I was getting pretty ordinary 2:2 marks for my essays. I carried out an experiment. I made a long list of about three hundred nouns and maybe about fifty adjectives and a sprinkling of verbs all culled from politics books borrowed from the university library. Armed with my cherry-picked political jargon I sat down to write my next essay. I answered the essay question using the same old Kit Fraser brain, with its same old second rate thought processes, employing the same tired old arguments; the only difference this time was that I was using new words. While implementing the language of political science I discovered two things. Not only did I find it easier to write the essays, but it actually served to refine my thinking on the subject and I got much better results.

On the other hand, I remember Professor Adam Morton, head of the philosophy department at Bristol University, who used to lecture in Canada, telling us that while the UK students were better educated and more articulate, generally speaking he felt that the Canadians' quality of thought was superior. He warned us against using verbal facility as a substitute for real thought. This is certainly not what I'm advocating. The author of the anonymous spiritual tome, *A Course In Miracles* writes: 'The arrogant must cling to words, afraid to go beyond them, to experience that which might affront their stance.' The skill of conversation is in finding words that do justice to your thoughts.

CHAPTER THREE

Friends

1 JOY NEEDS TO BE RECAPTURED

There are two schools of thought on the happiness question: expert opinion and my own private hunch. Psychologists say we are basically hard wired for unhappiness. Because we were designed to survive in nature, threatened on all sides by wild beasts and horrible lurgies, four out of our six primal emotions are necessarily negative, one is neutral and only one is positive. Our six universal emotions are:

> Anger – to deter aggressors.
> Fear – to alert us to danger.
> Disgust – to avoid contamination and therefore disease.
> Sadness – to make us cautious.
> Surprise – to incorporate life.
> Joy – to repeat what has worked.

I, however, think we are born happy. We never laugh so much in our lives as we do when we are children. We are never again so happy with so little, or have such a vast capacity for love. Julie the dog savaged my little daughter Vita's teddy bear, Tinkle, taking out its distinguishing features: its three buttons representing the teddy's nose and two eyes. So where there was a face, there was now a shocking hole with white wool gushing out. Vita was distraught, hugging the gruesome, faceless Teddy close to herself.

We quickly explained that Tinkle was injured but not dead and that we would buy her eyes and nose the following day and sew her face back together again. 'It's cosmetic surgery,' I explained. 'It's quite a common operation these days.' Then my son, Calum said:

'O look! I found one of Tinkle's eyes.' And Vita grabbed the button off him, put it on what remained of Tinkle's face and said with joy: 'Oh look! Tinkle can see again!'

I think we are born happy and life is a slippery slope. We are forever trying to get back to where we were. Geniuses and children are amazed by everything. Picasso said: 'I am amazed we don't melt in the bath like a bar of soap.'

2   OTHER PEOPLE ARE THE PROBLEM AND THE SOLUTION

Be that as it may, happiness expert and cognitive therapist, Dr Seligman recommends that to counteract the brain's nagging insistence on seeking out bad news, which was an aid to survival in the jungle but is now completely inappropriate in the comfort of modern life, you need to train yourself to be happy. He recommends four habits of mind:

1. Develop and retain positive memories of the past
2. Savour the present
3. Extract meaning out of activity
4. Make friends

Which of these four remedies is most effective? US self help guru Jack Black says: 'Personal relationships account for 85 per cent of our happiness but they also account for 85 per cent of our unhappiness too.'

I will give you two more lists from two other sources and you will notice what is common between these compilations of what it takes to be happy. First a list called the *Five Signs of Positive Life.*

1. Chattiness
2. Consideration
3. Particularity
4. Openness
5. Neurosis

I love the fifth requirement. There is no harm in neurosis. It gives grist to the mill. So don't go to a therapist. Don't waste your time gazing at your navel. Use your neurosis to make yourself interesting and entertaining. Your weaknesses, which your neurosis feeds on, are what make you open and accessible to friendship.

Another colour supplement list I have come across is *The Eight Aspects of Happiness*. The psychologist and author of this list said that schoolboy trickster William in the series *Just William* is the perfect prototype for somebody who is most likely to grow up happy. He displays all eight aspects that tend towards happiness.

1.   He is resourceful.
2.   Has good verbal skills.
3.   Is used to trouble.
4.   Is the leader of the pack.
5.   Has lots of friends and acquaintances.
6.   Is playful.
7.   Has the ability to immerse himself in a project.
8.   Has loving and supportive parents.

3   FRIENDSHIP IS NEXT TO GODLINESS

What all these lists of recommended behaviour have in common is firstly the paramount importance of friends; secondly the necessity of being good at talking; and thirdly the need to be attentive to whatever is happening.

There are two ways of approaching every single issue of life: spiritual and secular. It is surprising how they overlap. God's second commandment – the one immediately after insisting on devotion to Himself – is 'Love thy neighbour': a clarion call to friendship.

Jesus Christ himself, in his mission on earth, addressed us humble humans as friends. At no point in the Ten Commandments does he instruct you to love your wife. You have just got to be faithful to her. Perhaps this is because God realises that once the chemistry wears off, you are left with a feeling of affection much the same in character, if not degree, as any other friendship.

'I call you friends,' says Christ. Remember, he is supposed to be God made Man. It is like a king or an emperor tapping you on the shoulder and saying: 'Do you fancy a pint?' According to Jesus, friendship is the ideal relationship between people, not romantic love or admiration. He is not presenting himself as a star seeking adulation from his fans. He wants to be our friend.

The secular approach is as follows. The key question to ask an atheist or an agnostic is 'OK, what do you believe in?' Most people I know who don't believe in God do believe in family, friends, sex, alcohol, art, sport, or power. At different times and circumstances in your life, the order of preference changes. A high achiever would possibly put money and status at the top of his list. A widowed grandmother may prioritise her extended family but an adulterer obviously prefers sex. One was told by his doctor that he had to give up drink and he honestly said to me: 'Quite frankly I can't see the point of living anymore.' You don't want to underestimate these things just because they don't sound grand.

However, the way to work out your priorities is to imagine having to do without them and you will all come up with the same answer. We might not like it, but we can do without art, sport, alcohol, drugs, money, power, status, sex, drugs, rock and roll. Only loneliness is the killer. You cannot be happy without friends and incidentally, at the end of the day, once the romance has worn off, a wife is no more than a friend with sex.

The proof of the pudding is to see how you feel when you find yourself failing to connect with other people. All else seems unimportant: achievement, marriage, Third World suffering, money, God … everything. For all your apparent success in the world if you are lucky enough to have it, how sad it is to fail as I did at the Christmas works outing of my bar staff a few years ago. I realised I was more comfortable talking to a relative stranger, limited to introductory conversation, than immersing myself in the chaotic freedom of spontaneous banter as indulged in by my exuberant staff.

I came away from the night plunged in depression, feeling isolated and excluded. Nothing else mattered but that I should improve myself as a person so that in future I could take part in the freedoms my barmen and waitresses take for granted. OK, I am a lot older than my staff, but true freedom of expression should give you the ability to bridge age gaps, cultural differences and class barriers and I was disappointed in myself. It was one of the reasons I started to write this book.

4   AGE OFTEN INCREASES DISTANCE BETWEEN PEOPLE

There are lots of films illustrating this dilemma, like *About Schmidt* and *As Good as it Gets*. In both, Jack Nicholson plays an old curmudgeon lured out of his self-containment by unwilling contact with the outside world; yet as he discovers, there is no alternative to life except through other people, no matter how annoying they are.

Evelyn Waugh ended up as another old curmudgeon. In the famous 1953 BBC interview he was asked whether he had any close friends.

'One makes friends as one goes along,' he said. 'I'd say the bulk of my present friends are those I made at university. And then one quarrels perhaps twice a year and makes a new friend about once every two years.'

For most of us, school or university is the last time in our lives where we live in a village sized community and have the leisure, inclination and openness to make real friends in numbers. From then on in it is a precious rarity. It is a sad fact of most of our lives that the distance between us and other people increases as we get older. The film *Stand by Me* makes this depressing point. The narrator concludes that although he has not seen his school friends in thirty years, he has not made better friends since.

In *Stand by Me*, half a dozen boys set out on a weekend adventure.

Their imagination has been stirred by talk of murder. A body has been left to rot deep in a nearby forest. They all play truant and set out on an expedition to find it. The film is spent simply watching friendship at work as expressed in incidents of discussions, rows and arguments, mock mutual abuse, continuous teasing, playful rough-housing, joint ventures, shared oppressions, exchanged inadequacies, running jokes, rehashed common memories, uninterrupted time together, treats, inconveniences and discomforts – an endurance test. That is the definition of friendship.

What happens with some of us as we get older is that although we may well have developed a mannered social expertise, we stop taking the piss out of one another. This is where the working classes have the edge over the rest of us.

'A friend may well be reckoned the masterpiece of Nature,' said the philosopher Emerson. Yes, but what is it? What is friendship? In *Anam Cara,* John O'Donohue gives us the ten commandments of friendship, which also amount to a definition:

1.   Love begins with paying attention to one another.
2.   Break through the barriers of persona and egoism.
3.   Every friend goes through dark times.
4.   A real friend becomes part of you.
5.   Friendship is an act of reception and belonging.
6.   Love is the only way to judge somebody.
7.   The stranger does not come accidentally.
8.   A friend wakes you up to the wild possibilities within you.
9.   A friendship in difficulty needs a break.
10. The most precious thing in a friendship is the difference.

John O'Donohue says we are sent on this earth for one purpose only, 'to learn to love and to receive love.' It reminds me of the start of my second favourite musical, *Moulin Rouge,* where the young narrator makes a solemn vow to devote his life to the business of 'learning how to love and be loved in return.'

How do you make friends? Emerson says: 'by being one'. A fuller answer can be found in the slightly Machiavellian bestseller that practically single-handedly launched a new genre of literature known as self help-books, Carneggie's *How To Make Friends and Influence People.* His twenty-one point plan is:

1. Don't criticise people.
2. Appreciate them accurately.
3. Be aware of other person's needs and desires.
4. Be interested in what the other person is saying.
5. Smile.
6. Use the other person's name in conversation with him or her.
7. Listen.
8. Talk on the other person's subject.
9. Make the other person feel important.
10. Avoid arguments.
11. Use a friendly tone.
12. Get the other person to say yes.
13. Let the other person think an idea is theirs.
14. Be sympathetic to the other person's ideas.
15. Dramatise your ideas.
16. Throw down a challenge.
17. Praise before you correct a person.
18. Criticise indirectly.
19. Admit your own mistakes first.
20. Let the other person save face.
21. Give the other person a fine reputation to live up to.

5 WORDS ARE THE BRIDGE

You can have the fullest heart in the world, but if you can't get the *craic*, you are like a Brit abroad without his fellow Brits – lost, lonely and speechless. *Craic* is Gaelic for 'chat' and it is how in the Highlands of Scotland people are judged, as in 'Aye, he's good *craic*,' or, 'Aye, he's good at his job but he's no *craic*.'

This is one of the major points of the book. It is all very well God asking us to love thy neighbour as much as ourselves – so we are talking quite a lot of love – but arguably the only way to truly love somebody is to get them to love you too. Quite frankly, this is done most effectively by entertaining them in one way or another. Christianity, for all its pure intentions, is as power-dependent for its realisation as any other ideal.

Psychologists say that all relationships are conducted on an exchange and barter principle, which is why the most attractive and powerful people tend to gravitate towards one another. The subconscious question we are asking one another in the social market place is: 'What have you got to trade?' Product comes in the form of looks, wit and intellect. Obviously we assume the person is basically decent or we would probably not be considering him as potential for friendship. Goodness does not decide at what level in the social hierarchy we pair up with friends. In fact, very often goodness goes with power anyway. People tend to be good when they feel good.

6 WE ARE ALL IN THE ENTERTAINMENT BUSINESS

As D. H. Lawrence famously said, 'A man must be more than nice and good.' Boring people, for example, have a problem making friends. Of course there is no such thing as a completely boring person (although some people have an unnatural gift for concealing their entertainment value). At one end of the spectrum you have James Joyce who, according to the critic John Carey, 'was well known for treating everyone as equals whether they were writers, children, waiters, princesses or charladies. Their conversation always interested him. He had never, he said, met a bore.'

A more objective opinion on the subject comes from H. L. Mencken who observes: 'The capacity of human beings to bore one another seems to be vastly greater than any other animal. Some of their most esteemed inventions have no other apparent purpose – for example, the dinner party of more than two, the epic poem, and the science of metaphysics.' He is being funny with his examples but he is making a serious point. We live with the permanent threat of boredom. It dogs our every step; we put one foot wrong and, oh yes, once again we find our head in the noose of tedium and the trapdoor has just flipped open.

The worst insult is to call somebody boring. It is better to be called dishonest, inconsiderate, selfish or unfaithful. William Roache, who plays Ken Barlow of Coronation Street, bankrupted himself suing the *Sun* for calling him 'boring'. To be boring is everybody's worst nightmare and secret fear. If you accuse somebody of being boring you eliminate that person. There is no way back for that relationship. It is the worst insult because you are accusing the person of having aborted life's dual mission: to express themselves and to love. You cannot love without being loved and you cannot get anyone to love you if you are truly boring.

7 APPLAUSE DROWNS CHAT

What makes people boring? Fame is quite effective. Talk to the people who have experienced that phenomenon. It is incredibly debilitating because what we all try to do is to forget ourselves in the enjoyment of the moment – one of the blessings of alcohol, for example. Fame has the reverse effect. As the pop star Robbie Williams said about himself in the rock doc *Somebody Nobody*, fame makes you self-obsessed. As a result of thousands of interviews and a lifetime of the self-promotion necessary to achieve global success, apparently his conversational range is limited only to the subject of himself, at which he is an expert and really quite amusing.

Playwright Alan Bennett gave superb advice to the Rylstone WRI women who were suddenly thrust into the limelight with the publication of their nude calendar. 'Don't let fame go to your heads. Raspberry jam and Victoria sponge are far more important.'

8 BEWARE THE OFFICE

Work can make you dull. Not only that, it is dangerous. The adult environment of perpetual work and duty, of saying things you don't mean to people you would prefer not to be with, can start to put you off people.

Remember the nursery ditty: 'Too much work and not enough play makes Jack a dull boy.' This is particularly pertinent today, when chronic competition puts such steep demands on our workforce, especially with the high achievers amongst us. People do a lot of damage to themselves by being serious for thirty or forty years. They become irretrievable and end up facing the daunting prospect of a lonely old age because they have almost completely lost the ability to make new friends. As Evelyn Waugh points out, the old ones either fall out as a result of an irreparable quarrel or, as happens to me, gradually subside due to lack of connection.

Friends are formed by play. Any six-year-old knows that. Anybody else is a colleague or an acquaintance – enough common reference and data exchange to provide conversation for a brief encounter, but you are left with no real desire to see the person. It is not like my eight-year-old daughter who is sitting right now at the bottom of the garden waiting patiently to catch first sight of a car that will bring her best friend to play for the afternoon.

Yes, we all know there is a balance to be maintained between work and play, but I have seen lots of people, nearly all successful, who have lost themselves in their work and can't find themselves again when it is time to play. Derek Draper worked every day with Labour politician and self-confessed workaholic, Peter Mandelson. One day Draper suggested having dinner together with Mandelson.

'Peter quite literally didn't know what to do,' Draper reminisced in an interview. 'He neither needed me, nor needed to intimidate me – so there was no job to do over the course of the dinner. He was fidgeting, he couldn't cope. And I'm not joking. We sat down. We got some water. He looked at the menu. And he looked at me and said: "I'm sorry, I can't do this." And we left.'

The few people I know in the white-collar sector who have eschewed work for play tend either to be very rich or very poor. I notice they might not be particularly admirable – obviously lacking the work ethic, for example – but at least they have not lost the gift of friendship or the ability to enjoy a party. I have a neighbour who is a sculptor. She had some work commissioned by a multi-national company director and said that he was 'quite human for a suit'. Her automatic assumption was that a corporate man was most likely to be a bit of an automaton as there was inevitably a Faustian deal struck by anybody entering business life: your soul for your wallet.

9   AMBITION GOBBLES UP THE PRESENT

To get what you want you have to lose something. The solution is not to want anything. That is why monks and nuns don't want for anything. So their souls are not traded. Of course, in the outside world we do not have that privilege. We have to make commerce with mammon in order to provide for our families.

The answer, I suppose, is to limit your material ambitions as much as you can, but we are all prey to human nature which insists on more, more, more. The people who escape lightest are those people who realise their circumstances prevent any chance of success. Here the lowly-paid working men and women have the advantage over white-collar folk with their career structures offering them a chance to better themselves. If there is no prospect of promotion, you forget about the future and concentrate on having as good a time as possible with other people right now.

Postponement, projection and promotion are all aspects of bore-dom. W. H. Auden writes: 'People are born serious, selfish and honest. Through suffering, they must learn to become frivolous and insincere.' He means inventive, imaginative and creative – other words for experimenting with the truth, a form of positive lying – the lovely white lies of fiction.

Certain environments are not conducive to sparkling conversation. Quite frankly, a lot of modern life. In the TV documentary *Akenfield* all different types of people in the Suffolk village were interviewed about the changing times. 'What I notice most about the village is the way people no longer want to get together,' said Jobal Merton, a wheelwright by trade. 'All through my boyhood it was a regular thing for twenty or more folk to sit on that bank outside the shop and talk of an evening. They sat on the verge if it was fine and on the benches inside the shop if it was wet. The boys would be there too, rollocking and laughing but listening all the same. It was the good time of day and we all looked forward to it. We told each other about the things that happened to us, only a long time ago. We sang songs. We sang the army songs from the war like "Nellie Dean" and "Pack Up Your Troubles". Also the "Fakenham Ghost" and "The Farmer's Boy". And sometimes we step danced, although mostly the step dancing was done at Creningham "Bell". All that is finished now. People are locked in their houses with the television and haven't any more time for talk and the like.'

10   ANYTHING TO AVOID BEING BORING

I was halfway through a dinner party the other day when one of the guests suddenly said, out loud: 'I just want to go home.' Social discomfort got the better of him. He was over fifty, yet the five-year-old in him had sprung to his lips. 'I feel so boring,' he amazingly admitted to me. 'And you're so at ease with all this.'

'Not really,' I replied, 'I'm just pissed.' And then I said, by way of comforting him, 'But I'm so envious of the easy *craic* you have with your hunting friends and office partners.'

'Oh,' he said, 'we're not that friendly.' And then he paused. 'Is everyone insecure?' he said. His humility made me feel a lot better about by myself. It is good to know that other people are often not having a better time than you, even if they look as if they are.

Mind you, I can do one better than him. You should see me at a Scottish ball, which I have had to attend on an annual basis through most of my life. What does it feel like to be boring? Here is my experience at the Northern Meeting Ball in 2005, lifted verbatim from my diary and numbered, as is my wont.

1. Lone individual skirting groups and couples of happily chatting revellers. The social leper.
2. People excusing themselves from your company: left, right and centre. Suddenly they have to go to the bar or the toilet or find their partners for the next dance.
3. Bridie comes up to me in the middle of a set and says I look: 'shell-shocked'.
4. Kate Rous telling me to stop yawning when I was only coughing.
5. Standing opposite somebody stunned with boredom, thinking how can I take this stuttering exchange one syllable further?
6. Then later in the night at four in the morning, you get that yearning-for-bed feeling when you finally peel off your kilt stockings and steam actually rises from your compressed legs.
7. The leaden conversations going nowhere that neither of you want or for the slightest moment believe in.
8. And then the dozen stars amongst the four hundred. These are the kings to whom the rest of us are either courtiers or courtesans. These guys are never at a loss for a word. They are full of masculine grace. They smile and laugh with happy ease. Actually nearly everybody seems to be enjoying themselves except for you and maybe a couple of other total losers who would quite frankly be happier digging a ditch.

9. The feeling of wonder. What on earth is everyone talking about when there is patently nothing to say? If only I didn't have to talk, I would be quite happy.

10. Breakfast is the high point of the evening. Unbelievably they haven't ballsed up the scrambled eggs. You try and do scrambled eggs for four hundred! There's black pudding and potato scones, rashers of bacon, two bloody good fat sausages and a fried tomato. The whole thing excellently done.

11. Now back to the dance floor on a full stomach but still the same empty feelings. No camaraderie amongst fellow social weaklings, just a tremendous antipathy based on an appalling mutual recognition. 'God, I'm as dull as that. Socially speaking I'm in the Vauxhall League.' That's football parlance for not very good. The horrific thing is that at the bottom end of social performance, you can arrive at a full stop – a juddering halt. I'm talking noises rather than words.

12. Then there is the booze option where you try and kick start your mind with alcohol. This will not work if you are not in the mood. Where you were anonymous now you are merely advertising your social incompetence because you feel all dammed up inside, the alcohol merely increases the pressure and you discover your face heating up like a boiled cabbage, your shirt hangs out and for some unknown reason your hair goes all skew-whiff. What you say when you do talk is the stuff of simpletons.

13. The really sad thing is dull people know they are dull and have known it all their lives through ten thousand interminable social events and yet – and this is the incredible thing – they still go, to be once again painfully reminded how second rate they are. I really take my hat off to these people. Is it hope over experience or is it just stoicism? Very often these people are great in a time of war.

What is the cure of boredom? 'You're never bored when you're pished!' is an old Highland saying: speaking as a pub owner, and so a beneficiary of those people who have taken that option, it certainly has got a lot to recommend it, but one assumes that after a while the bad outweighs the good. The real cure for boredom is to learn how to talk and listen well. That has an immediate knock-on effect on how you feel and think. It is a virtuous circle.

11 ENCYLOPEDIAS ARE BORING

You don't have to be a great brain to converse well with your neighbour. Very often the brain is an obstacle because the bloody thing throws up too many options, too many qualifying clauses, too many tangents. The great philosopher Frederick Nietzsche, for example, could barely string a sentence together in conversation. No, you don't want too much brain, although you need enough of one to be able to stay on a subject for a while.

Having said that, thinking that allows you to cross reference between subjects and skate lightly over topics, if done with intelligence, can be highly effective in company. Verticality, the ability to delve deep into a subject, might be good for your career, but different rules apply in the pub and the drawing room. This explains how great thinkers can be crap conversationalists.

12 GREAT SOCIALITES NEED SAY VERY LITTLE

And there is nothing more deadly than having to listen to an authority on a subject. You are far better watching a documentary or reading a book. It is not power of thought or even refinement of feeling that makes a person fun to be with. It is just how exquisitely they dance attendance on you while being utterly themselves. That is the magic formula.

Some of the most charismatic people you meet socially say nothing of note. You feel they are fascinating but afterwards you cannot repeat a word of what they have said. This is the point Anthony

Blanche makes to Charles Ryder about the oh-so-charming Lord Sebastian Flyte, the toast of Oxford University, in *Brideshead Revisited.* Anthony Blanche says: 'Tell me candidly have you ever heard Sebastian say anything you have remembered for five minutes? You know, when I hear him talk, I am reminded of that in some ways nauseating picture of "Bubbles". Conversation should be like juggling: up go the balls and the plates, up and over, in and out, good solid objects that glitter in the footlights and fall with a bang if you miss them. But when dear Sebastian speaks it is like a little sphere of soapsuds drifting off the end of an old clay pipe, anywhere, full of rainbow light for a second and then – phut! Vanished, with nothing left at all, nothing.'

Pure envy because it is Sebastian, not Anthony, who holds the secret of social charm in conversation. Indeed we learn a few paragraphs later that Charles 'sat immobile and almost silent throughout the entire evening' listening to Anthony's tirade against the Flytes and pontifications about art. Anthony's eloquence amuses, interests and finally oppresses Charles. It is Sebastian who charms him. The performer cannot compete with the person. You can enjoy a show. You can't have a relationship with it, and Anthony is just show.

Sebastian has different problems, which exacerbate as he gets older. He is an extreme example of someone who dreads himself. He feels himself in a state of sin due to his homosexuality, and he dreads other people for their tedious conventionality. As an English Oxbridge Catholic aristocrat – best race, best university, best religion, best class – the twit was a hell of an elitist, but they were twittish times. Anyway this attitude of chronic superiority put him off most people. Drink blots out everybody including himself and he ends up with God for company.

13 LONELINESS IS A GREAT SPUR TO HAPPINESS

People tend either to in some degree dread themselves or other people, and that determines their level of sociability. The great thing about dreading yourself is that wherever you can, you seek to avoid your own company, which makes you very sociable. The beautiful model Caroline Eicholtz says: 'I feel sad that I always need to be surrounded by people to feel happy.'

This remark of hers tallies with the results of a survey reported in *The Sunday Times* on October 2nd 2005, which found that sociability is the prime requirement for personal happiness. 'The top ten per cent of very happy people found they spent the least time alone and the most time socialising,' the article said. By that the survey is not referring to the top ten per cent of all very happy people, but the ten per cent of all happy people who happen to be happiest. Don't you love the solemn statistics and the mathematical certainties of these experts? It's sweet.

Why is socialising the most effective way of being happy? Because we are dancing animals, says US cult novelist Kurt Vonnegut. 'Walking to the post, talking to other human beings, having relationships in real physical spaces rather than virtual ones, is such fun, so why not do it? We are dancing animals.'

From either end of the spectrum of conventional morality I give you Lord Byron and Our Lady. They are both in agreement as to the importance of people meeting to get the *craic*. Lord Byron had nothing but contempt for stay-at-home people. These so-called respectable people might have called him a wastrel, but he reckoned it was they who were wasting their lives tucked up safe and sound. Our Lady, through the visionaries of Medjugorje, has told us to make communion either directly to God through prayer, or indirectly through conversation with one another, for a minimum of three hours a day.

We are sorely failing to carry out Our Lady's instructions here in Scotland, where according to the latest statistics we spend just forty-seven and a half minutes a day socialising compared to the three hours a day we spend watching TV and surfing the internet. Incidentally we help other people for just eight minutes a day. Jean

Vanier of L'Arche, an international faith community, thinks sharing meals with other people is important for our spiritual welfare. He says we should aim to get through a sack of salt in a lifetime.

CHAPTER FOUR

Self

1 YOU ARE MADE UP OF HABITS

Our capacity to make friends diminishes with age. Work, social and domestic routines result in not only a reductive particularisation of the mind – so lawyers tend primarily to knock around with other lawyers, toffs with toffs, football fans with football fans – but also, because of the breakdown of community and the million distractions of contemporary life, the necessary stillness needed for real connection is all but gone.

A distance crops up between you and other people. Increasingly you find yourself staying at arms length rather than immersing yourself in the other person and what is being said. You get the rise of the alienated individual, the solitary soul compensating for his loneliness with hours a day watching telly and networking on the internet.

Even those of us who maintain as full a social life as our energies allow can often feel like spectators rather than participants in the dance of friendship. A hardening mould forms around you with age, but this mould can be broken by harnessing power available to you in the spoken word. That vital focus will transform your life, but it does require huge personal effort. The rewards kick in almost immediately, but unlike chasing money, the joy of talk cannot be easily quantified. And it all seems terribly unnatural, but conversation is an art form and so needs plenty of work if you want to get good at it. We are all artists. What we attempt to do when we talk to one another is exactly the same as a novelist in his writing. We seek to express ourselves as effectively as possible and in such a way as to produce the desired effect on the person or people on the receiving end.

3 WHO ARE YOU?

In order to express yourself, first of all you need to know who you are. What is 'self'? You can talk about 'personality', which is a projection of self. Then there is 'character', which is an expression of self, and what I call 'The Second Self', which speaks to you in the small voice of intuition.

That little inner voice is audible only if you are truly attentive and prepared to dare the truth. A lot of people are bold in telling the truth about other people, but are cowards about themselves. Lies are lethal to self. They silence its voice. You have got to get used to being merciless about the truth no matter what the consequences, no matter how damaging to your self-esteem. You must not merely protect yourself.

Convention cramps the self. Just because everybody else thinks in a certain way is no reason why you should. Don't let anybody else think for you. Majority opinion is wrong for you, even when it is right. 'Either you think – or others have to think for you and take power from you, prevent and discipline your natural tastes, civilise and sterilise you,' writes Scott Fitzgerald in *Tender is the Night*.

4 YOU ARE ORIGINAL

Learn to listen to your real self. It is original. Children are in touch with their Second Selves and look how original they are. 'Out of the mouths of babes,' we say. They think for themselves and so must you. It can be the most incidental of thoughts. For example it occurred to me out of the blue the other day that Hamlet was gay. I then went through the play with a fine tooth comb, searching for evidence. In thinking outside the box, I found nuances I never would have appreciated if I wasn't actively stretching the boundaries of my assumptions.

5 DREAMS PROVE THE EXISTENCE OF THE SECOND SELF

Dreams are evidence that the Second Self exists, as Freud and Jung realised. Have you ever had a dream where other people in it seem to know more than you do and yet the whole dream is a product of your own mind? It is like a novelist not knowing as much as one of his fictional characters.

I will give you a couple of revealing dreams I've had – one to do with personal exposure and the other a classic about persecution. This first was a simple one about a karaoke night at a Scottish wedding reception where I was in a dress kilt. I got on stage and performed an Elvis impersonation to huge laughter and applause.

Only after the performance was I told that the apparent success of my performance was actually ridicule. The audience could see I was wearing nothing under my kilt, which became apparent in my wild rock'n'roll gyrations. The crowd, a figment of my imagination, knew more than I did and I was the author of the dream!

The second dream was a stitch up. I was walking round a National Trust property. It was an old monastery that had been turned into a school. There were a couple of uniformed doormen who asked me to empty my pockets. Amazingly, I pulled out a bundle of stuff including a handkerchief, Blu-Tack, conkers and about four or five marbles. The door staff let me through although they appeared to be highly suspicious of me for no apparent reason.

Then out of the blue I got a random erection, as you can in dreams, not induced by any sexual thought at all. Obviously I had to conceal it and I pretended to have a pain in my stomach and rushed for a seat in order to wait for the erection to die down. Suddenly, I was arrested for paedophilia. They realised I had an erection and the conkers and marbles apparently proved I was intent on grooming youngsters.

What is interesting about the dream is that it showed I was not in charge of the story. The story knew stuff I didn't. I didn't know why the conkers and marbles caused such consternation at the door until later when the door staff had put two and two together after having discovered my concealed erection. I did not even know why there had to be door staff in the first place. It was a classic Kafka dream with the innocent proven guilty: the evidence that had evolved in the course of the dream was put together and interpreted by other characters, only being explained to the author of the dream at the end.

Incidentally, do you ever have dreams where you are left out of the conversation because you are not clever or witty enough to take part and you stand there amazed at other people's brilliance? But their marvellous conversation is actually coming out of your head because it is your dream!

6   HOW TO ACCESS YOUR SECOND SELF

There are all sorts of ways of accessing your Second Self: hypnosis, meditation, prayer, drink, love, recreational drugs … The rosary works by occupying the surface of your mind with the mechanical business of reciting The Hail Mary fifty times so as to free up your Second Self. C. S. Lewis wrote in his book *Chiefly on Prayer*: 'A clergyman once said to me that a railway compartment, if one has it to oneself, is an extremely good place to pray in because there is just the right amount of distraction.'

I recommend mindlessly boring repetitive office work because it also allows your real spirit to come through, like grass in the cracks between paving stones. That is how shyness and self-consciousness are defeated in the world of work. It is the other reason why love and friendship flourish at the work place. How is it you can suddenly say that someone is your friend? There is no event, like a kiss on the lips, to tell you something has happened in the relationship. It is just a feeling you get that your Second Selves have made contact. Suddenly you are talking for real to one another. You are in communion.

8 SO DOES REPARTEE

Watch those amazing comedians on the telly. How on earth do they do it? Where do they get their spontaneous brilliance? You occasionally come across people with a quick sense of repartee in your social life and we all admire them and what fun they have. Their secret, which has become second nature to them, is that early on in their development they acquired the habit of accessing their Second Self while not abandoning their First Self. It is a balancing act like riding a bicycle.

Those who exclusively inhabit the First Self must live purely by force of will and a slavish adherence to the norm while other people, especially writers and thinkers, delve deep into their minds and never fully re-emerge. So they too lose their equilibrium. They are more comfortable in their Second Self. They become increasingly de-socialised, much to their chagrin. Beware the desert, for it can put you off the marketplace and vice versa. Too much time dwelt in the Second Self and you can lose touch with the easy knack of social exchange that requires use of the surface of your mind.

10 KEEP A JOURNAL OF MYSTERY MOMENTS

Your Second Self has its own special memory and whatever it chooses to remember, especially if it is apparently trivial, carries a payload of significance for you personally. First you need to make yourself aware of its existence and then be alert to its every utterance, its every sign of life and its every souvenir. Freud and Jung have taught us the value of dreams. Their advice is to record and then analyse them to develop our understanding of ourselves.

Memories are equally revealing. We forget 99.9 per cent of our lives. So the tiny bit we do remember is significant. Why do we remember what we do? Obviously we remember major events but, much more interestingly, we also remember certain apparent trivia.

Why? Because these nuggets of information somehow resonate with our own unique psyche.

That is why I recommend keeping a Journal of Mystery Moments. If you do that, you will be astonished at the subsequently meaningful and indeed prophetic quality of stuff you might not recognise at the time as being in any way important. I have got hundreds of Mystery Moments recorded in my journal and each one, no matter how mundane, I can interpret. I will give you three or four examples.

Here is a pertinent example. Years before I realised the importance of keeping journals, I read Isobel Colegate's novel *The Shooting Party*. For some odd reason, the only thing I could subsequently remember of this excellent book was the scene when a little girl comes across her grandfather at his desk, keeping up his daily diary. She asks him what he's doing and he says, 'Oh, I'm just keeping a diary. It's where I keep my thoughts so I don't have to bother anybody else with them.'

Similarly, why is it that of all the things I have read about Napoleon, the one thing that really sticks in my mind is that as a young man on holiday he used to picnic on hills, wondering how he would lay siege to the towns below? That is exactly my attitude to pubs now they are my livelihood. I sit there drinking a pint, imagining how I would make them work properly. Most pubs are insolvent but for the truly heroic endeavours of the management and staff.

An old business colleague of my father's once said to me, when I was maybe eleven, 'Never lose that laugh and you will succeed.' It is only now, forty years later, that I realise that he was right. Fun is not created by the person telling a joke, but by the recipient who sets up the situation and allows it to flourish.

Do you know what the funniest man in print, A. A. Gill, says about funny people? 'Almost everyone involved in comedy is bereft of a sense of humour. That is, they're not funny and have no sense of what humour is. It's the audience that has the sense of humour.

We feed them.' It is the king not the clown who rules the court, and the man who laughs is really the king.

Similarly, the key to business is listening not talking – and if you can do that while making the other person feel clever, interesting and amusing you really will succeed. The point is that although at the time my conscious mind dismissed my father's friend's advice, my Second Self chose to store his precious little tip until such time as I was ready to appreciate the full import of his observation – particularly relevant to an over-performer like myself who needs to correct that imbalance within himself and attend more to other people.

Why is it that in the whole of Scottish history, the bit that most sticks in my mind is when Robert the Bruce on his little hill pony slays the charging armour-clad knight, Henry de Bohun, with a deft stroke of his humble axe just before the historic battle of Bannock-burn. While the uproarious cheers of his assembled army are ringing in his ears, all he says is, 'I have broken my good axe.' Success has its price. It may look small but it isn't. What you lose with fame, money and power is the ability to appreciate the concrete and a lessening in your connection with other people. Obviously I have achieved very little of that unholy trinity of success, but even I can see I have lost certain appreciations when I compare myself to my bar staff.

Isn't it surprising that these apparently minor moments seem to be imprinted for ever on my mind? The television serialisation of the book *Brideshead Revisited* had a huge effect on contemporary university undergraduates of my vintage, yet the one bit of the entire twelve hours of delicious film that stayed to haunt me was the moment when Sebastian Flyte shows how reluctant he is to intro-duce his friend, Charles Ryder, to the rest of his family. He is honest enough to explain that he dreads Charles Ryder preferring them to him. Decades later I discovered precisely the same feeling in myself when several years into my marriage I started to be wary of intro-ducing newly acquired friends to my wife, who had blossomed into an amazing woman. I had started to dread them preferring her to me.

The list of telling memories goes on and I won't bore you with any more of them. I would just recommend you make a list of your own and as long as you give your internal memory free rein, a lot will be revealed to you about yourself.

11 FEED THE SECOND SELF. STARVE DEPRESSION!

You know how you have to shake a bottle of real orange juice to mix up the sediment with the rest of the liquid to get it nice and drinkable? Well that's exactly what you have to do with the sludge that can settle in the pit of your mind if it is not in a permanent state of animation, so that where there was mechanical existence now there is life.

'Rage, rage against the dying of the light,' writes Dylan Thomas in his famous poem about the need to resist death at all times, even if you are old and decaying. The light he is talking about is not just daylight, but the light of your mind. This is what dims when the spirit is depressed and overcome with feelings of emptiness, loneliness and helplessness – what I call the three Loch Ness Monsters.

Machines offering us immediate distraction at the cost of a more immediate connection have reduced our energy levels at best, if not plunged us into an incapacitating inertia. In just a decade from 1991 to 2002 we in this country have doubled the number of anti-depressant prescriptions we take. So if the drugs are being administered correctly, then we are twice as sad as we used to be. If the current rate continues, within a century there will hardly be a happy person left in the UK!

I kid you not. In 2002 doctors made out twenty-two million prescriptions. How many prescriptions does a sad person take out a year? Let's hope it is a lot because if it is not, it means unhappiness in the UK is reaching epidemic proportions. What is particularly concerning for me is that depression in Scotland is 40 per cent higher than in England. This I put down to Presbyterianism, which is very depressing for the majority of us who are not members. The rest of us, according to Scotland's national religion, are doomed to go to hell, no matter how well we behave; also depressing.

Combine that gloomy prospect with the dark, cold Scottish winter and it is no wonder by early February you find yourself loitering by the medicine cabinet, covetously eyeing pots of pills. Then you are saved by the very religion that induces those dangerous feelings of unworthiness in the first place and you say to yourself: 'what's the rush? Life might be bad but why make things worse?'

The second funniest line in literature* is about Scots' weak hold on happiness. It comes from P. G. Wodehouse, who once famously wrote: 'It is easy to tell the difference between a Scotsman with a grudge and a ray of sunshine.' Not that I am one to crow: I will come out of my closet and admit to my Scottish background. I too do not do joy although I can rustle up the occasional chuckle when the occasion demands it. However, my normal state of mind is a middling mild melancholia.

What is the spirit? It is what can so easily die in a millionaire. It is what is dead in a porn star. 'I've never met a happy porn star,' says Traci Lords, author of a book called *Underneath It All* about the US sex industry. It's what you lose forever when you do something irretrievable like murder someone. Adultery gobbles it up as well. Incidentally, the whole point of prayer is to feed it.

Spirit is that buoyancy. It is the child who forever plays in a man's heart - the thing within us that makes us laugh outright or gives us the giggles, the little Mexican bean that is in all of us somewhere. In later life it often gets replaced by a pleasure inducing

* The funniest is when Bertie Wooster has taken the opportunity to grow a moustache when Jeeves is away on holiday and, indicating the growth on his upper lip, Wooster greets Jeeves with the words: 'I have not been idle while you have been away!'

form of sedation called complacency. We actively and consciously try and bring him out to play in our social life, but he is often suffocated by worldly calculation. The little fella normally likes a drink and television puts him to sleep but, worst of all, if starved of daily sustenance he becomes depressed, which is the Latin word for being pushed down.

This book is an attack on depression. It is a worthy enemy. The statistics are hideous. A fifth of us will suffer a severe depressive episode in our lives. 87 per cent of people suffering depression are not treated for it. Three million people in this country at any one time suffer from depression. More than half these people will consider suicide, so that means right now one and a half million people in this country want to kill themselves. Thankfully there is a huge difference between wanting and doing. Only 150,000 of them actually attempt suicide per year.

Depression can come from the pain or discomfort of illness, bereavement, lack of sunlight, stress, neurosis, low self esteem, unemployment, debt, frustration in the work place, bad or broken relationships, childbirth, abuse of alcohol and drugs etc. There are four hundred recognised types of psychotherapy – the best known being Gestalt Therapy, which prioritises games playing; Trans-actional Therapy, which concentrates on role play; and Cognitive Therapy, which seeks to dispel mistaken or deluded thinking by reason and recommends changes in mental habits.

I agree totally with these talk-based remedies: change of habits and the importance of play are central to the message of this book, but purpose is the other half of the story. 'When I am depressed I am totally bored by other people's conversations,' observes John Cornwell, who writes extensively about the subject. People are visited by a huge feeling of *what is the point of what you are saying?* Which quickly becomes *what is the point of anything?*

God helps there, because if you believe in Him at least you have a point: spiritual salvation. But how can a rational person really believe? Religion is the opposite of common sense. It is a kind of madness. Love your enemy. Somebody slaps you across the cheek and you are supposed to offer him the other one. Eat my body. Drink my blood. The meek are cool. And as for Jesus' famous cry from the cross – 'Why have You abandoned me?' – are we really expected to devote our lives to a guy whose penultimate words indicate that he has been dumped by his number one backer?

He would not last a moment in business. And not only are we supposed to love somebody we have never seen, we have also got to talk to him on a regular basis. Prayer is talking to God but so is conversation, the subject of this book.

12   HAPPINESS IS A BALANCE BETWEEN YOUR TWO SELVES

So to recap: one of the two main purposes in life is to express yourself, but to do that you need to know who you are. Your personality is on show for all to see and you can have an idea of yourself by the way other people react to you. Then there is your character, which is revealed when times get out of hand and you can see how you behave under pressure such as in a marriage. Clues are given about your subconscious or Second Self in dreams and memories. They tell you about your psychic self. This is the core of your being and the job of life is to marry your upper and lower selves or, to put it another way, to have your conscious mind in perfect alignment with your subconscious. A sign that you are bringing this off – and everybody succeeds on occasion – is when you have completely forgotten yourself and you are immersed in the moment. It is one of the reasons people drink. It can temporarily free yourself and allow your Second Self to come to the surface and have a good time.

A sign that your two selves are in a state of harmony is that you discover you have found your voice. You relate to your inner world through thought. If these thoughts are not your own thoughts, then they are second hand thoughts.

13 WE ARE ALL BRILLIANT

In order to find your own voice, you need to have your own thoughts, but that certainly does not mean you should stop listening to other people. Don't worry about acting like a cuckoo. You can lay your eggs in other peoples' nests. Be shameless. Beg, steal and borrow other peoples' thoughts, ideas and phrases, but then put them through the filter of your own mind. Put them down in your diary, articulate them for yourself and get to own them. By doing that, you are creating your own collage. A sentence is made up of words, not one of which you have invented, but the composition is yours. Similarly, you can borrow other peoples' thoughts and percolate them through your own unique experience and so personalise them.

As discussed earlier, we are all capable of fascinating insights and great stories. My journals are as full of telling quotes from ordinary people as from celebrated authors, thinkers and performers. What your Aunt Maggie has just said can be as stimulating as anything issuing from the mouth of Einstein himself. Quite frankly, the only difference between any of us and a great novelist, for example, is stamina. As the brilliant modern American novelist, Kurt Vonnegut, said: 'If a person with a demonstrably ordinary mind, like mine, will devote himself to giving birth to a work of imagination, that work will in turn tempt and tease that ordinary mind into cleverness.' Ernest Hemingway said: 'A failure to write a novel is just a failure of character.'

And there's nothing wrong with a little bit of bollocks. It leavens the yeast of truth. The other day I was riveted by what Ong, our Thai head waiter, told me about his father's guru who is a Buddhist monk aged about 104. This monk made the following twenty-one statements. How can you resist them? Some are ordinary, some extraordinary, some fascinating, but the list would die on the page without the rubbish. What was repeated to me via Ong's father to Ong was as follows:

1. Everyman should do a fortnight in the jungle without food.
2. Certain Buddhas you cannot shoot. The bullet just goes round them.
3. If you know the system, you can fly.
4. There are 227 rules, two of which are no alcohol and no sex.
5. Religion is impossible without fasting.
6. Free yourself from physical craving.
7. Trees have power.
8. Talk to your plants.
9. Hormones rule.
10. Oxygen is essential.
11. Blood comes in two colours: black and red.
12. Heat purifies the blood.
13. Liver and kidney removes pollutant.
14. Cucumbers are deadly.
15. In your diet you need a balance of colours.
16. Broccoli is good for cancer.
17. Herbs are powerful.
18. Meditating is not boring.
19. Acupuncture is bad.
20. Pills are counterproductive.
21. Barefoot gives you power from the ground.

If I am ever burgled in my house, I will set about the thief with a cucumber and that will show him.

CHAPTER FIVE

Culture

1 DISTINGUISH REALITY FROM NORMALITY.
HARDLY ANYONE DOES.

Why is it so important to think for yourself? Apart from the fact that not doing so lands you in the soup – think of the credit crunch, or the expenses scandal – following the pack simply does not lead to good conversation. Parrots are not great conversationalists.

Why do we tend not to think for ourselves? It is because the vast majority of us believe in normality, not reality. T. S. Eliot famously said that we can't cope with much reality. It is too devastating. Normality happens with consensus. And we find this totally acceptable up until the time when somebody points out that the emperor is not wearing any clothes. If you do dare to think for yourself, you have to actively seek the reality of a situation, which is no easy feat. But those who make the effort are more interesting, and more charismatic people.

2 TREAT ART LIKE FOOD

The key to opinion is self. Treat, for example, art like food. I do not have to consult a restaurant guide to be able to tell you with complete confidence that I don't like beetroot. It should be the same with novels, paintings and music because that is the only way to progress. If you find James Joyce's *Ulysess* verbose, chronically self-indulgent and boring as fuck, it's a crime to sit around a dinner party agreeing how brilliant it is. That puts the stopper on you. It blocks your development. You may climb the ladder of appreciation by going from one rung of knowledge to the next but first and foremost, the thing you need to know is yourself: what you genuinely feel about what you are considering. Then you need to find the words to articulate your reaction and your reasons. For this second part you can take advice, possibly in the form of education.

This is the message in the film *Educating Rita*. The professor is so relieved to come across Rita, a breath of fresh air compared to his other students, who are all conventional products of the educational system. Rita thinks for herself even if her form of expression is quite crude. She makes the connection between Shakespeare and life. She was a frustrated housewife unfulfilled by her working class environment, wanting more than jolly gossip and limited material aspiration.

She came at the arts with a vengeance. Her mind had not been straitjacketed by the examination system. Education is wasted on the young. Rita is the right age – about thirty, with a good dollop of life experience under her belt – so she knows what Shakespeare was talking about even if she was a little short on vocabulary. By comparison, her classmates were just going through the motions. Their essays expressed conventional opinion couched in appropriate language designed ultimately to qualify them to take their rightful place in the establishment. The corporate system only wants original thinkers at the very top. The vast majority of white collar people are just processors of information.

You don't want too many chiefs. In fact, you only want two of them: the managing director and the chairman. The rest need to be Indians: lawyers, accountants, salesmen, administrators and middle management, carrying out the bosses' instructions.

That is what you want for an organisation, but what is right for the group can be wrong for the individual. The corporation can give you money and status and community but it takes your time, your mind and if you are not careful, your actual identity. You must seek to retain something of yourself. Serial killer Dr Harold Shipman was aware of this when he started his life prison sentence. 'The problem is for thirty years I've had the professional mask of a doctor. Now I'm me. Who am I?' he moaned.

3 YOUR ACCENT IS YOUR HOME

Beware anybody whose accent changes depending on whom they are with. Watch the people who have phone voices. I know, for example, a woman whose voice always changed to accommodate her latest boyfriend. Her affairs were conducted with impeccable discretion. So her misbehaviour went unnoticed to the naked eye, but was obvious to the discerning ear. I knew precisely when there was a change of personnel. When the charming Irish musician made way for the perfect English gent, out went 'top of the morning' and in came 'OK yah'.

When eventually all was revealed to her doting husband and the whole edifice of her social life came crashing about her ears, she felt impelled to go to an expensive therapist to find out who she was. She did not have a clue, even though she was in her mid-forties; like the great geisha girl that she was, she was not herself but a reflection or a projection of whatever her current man desired. At Magdalene, Samuel Pepys observed that the fellows of his old college spoke in new voices; they had abandoned the puritan twang he remembered from his undergraduate days. The Puritans were out and the king was in, so their accents changed accordingly.

Staying rooted in the heart of your community greatly helps in finding out who you are. So when somebody changes their accent it is an obvious sign that they are losing sight of where they come from. That is one of the drawbacks of being sent away to boarding school. Loss of a regional accent shows a void. It describes the absence from home. This premature departure causes a loss of identity. It opens up a hollowness that forever more needs to be filled, which makes for an almost perfect environment to create high achievers. Hence the outstanding success of this privileged educational system, which turns happy little children into hollow high achievers seeking to fill that gap in themselves with food, drink, drugs, money, sex, success, activity and distraction.

It has made this tiny island a world beater because there never was a ruling elite so ill at ease with itself. Excellent for action. These agitated, self flagellating, greedy and sentimental idealists created an Empire (to their credit, they gave it back with comparative civility) and then went on to win a couple of world wars.

4 ACHIEVEMENT IS COMPENSATION

Happy people don't push themselves to succeed because they are having too good a time with their friends. What you want to do is burrow a hole in somebody's insides and then he will spend the rest of his life trying to fill it up, trying to earn other people's love, admiration and respect, like Sir Lancelot with phenomenal acts of derring do because at too early an age the little prep school boy was robbed of his calm.

There is a tension, a nervousness to these boys later in adult life, which lurks just beneath the surface of their studied social poise. It is why the most mundane thing delivered in an accent by a working man has a resonance and energy lacking in the neutral tones of somebody speaking with received pronunciation.

Stand up comedy is our bullfighting. It's the bravest thing we do. It is one man and a microphone pitted against the crowd – one man daring to outwit the people. One false move and he's dead. The hecklers scent blood and the rest of us are embarrassed. I tried it once, just to see what it was like. It was terrifying. Why is it that all our stand-up comics are accented? Because a voice that is neutered by education lacks the necessary impetus. You need more than a microphone to dominate a room. You need an accent for power, as well as a brain for wit. Toffs have to compensate. They need all the education they can get.

5 CULTURE COMES FROM PLACE

As important as where you come from is where you are going to. With the passage of time this will also determine who you are, or at least who you are becoming because what happens in life is you become what you want. If those ends are selfish, you will become selfish. If they are money-orientated, you will become money-orientated. If your aim in life is to get on with people, you will get on with them. If your aim is noble, you will become noble. As the Jewish saying goes: 'Beware of what you want for you may surely get it!'

Of course, most people's aims are a mixture, which is why we tend to be a little mixed up ourselves. Sometimes I am almost pious in my intentions and other times frankly quite lecherous, depending on the situation. If you put a naked woman in front of me I don't feel very religious. It's all a question of what you allow to be put in front of you.

A healthy culture teaches us to put the right things in front of us. It teaches us to distinguish gold from glitter. It makes us realise in advance what is important. We should not devote our lives to something as foolish as money, for example. I say foolish because, of course, money is merely a means to an end. It's silly to make the means an end in itself! It used to be the culture of the British upper classes never to discuss money in a social situation. It was considered the height of bad form. No gentleman would dream of such a lapse in manners.

Now that we have been to a large extent Americanised, all that has changed. Worse still, now that society is dispersed (or according to Margaret Thatcher, actually ceased to exist) we have the cult of the individual. Television puts the little fellow on a pedestal. Reality TV gives everybody their quarter of an hour, as predicted by Andy Warhol decades ago. Without society we are unfortunately left to our own devices. We no longer know how to behave. No amount of self-help books will give you culture. Bookworms don't make writers because culture, like writing, comes from life, not reading about it.

T. S. Eliot argues that a writer is a channel for culture. So Shakespeare and Dickens are not themselves 'culture', only products of culture. They are the product of the interaction between man and experience, which most immediately expresses itself in language. Experience comes in two forms: activity and environment. Somebody who has been taken from his home environment is immediately at a disadvantage. The joy of real culture is it makes the pursuit of money and power seem a waste of time. A truly cultured person prefers a happy chat with a friend to the purchase of that person's time or the control of that person. In my bar, the staff have ten times the fun than I have and yet I own it and employ them.

6   CULTURE GIVES YOU POWER

Another point of culture is to prevent you talking like a salesman or an administrator or any other talk professional. Culture should bring out the real you with your own real voice within the bosom of your community. That is why salesmen and bureaucrats sound ridiculous to the working man who has daily physical connection with matter – one of the three compound elements of reality, or the creative intellectual who has an animate connection with information, or anyone of spirit who uses energy to positive effect – the other two elements. Real laughs at fake. Sales talk and bureaucratic bullshit are fake. Culture is real.

Classically a sign of culture is someone who is capable of holding you in their thrall without ever saying very much. Powerful people need to say very little to cast a spell over you. They are like the finest matadors who barely move to avoid the horns of the bull as it bears down upon them, or the truly great comics like Tommy Cooper whose material was as lame as a duck and yet could still render you helpless with laughter.

7 SELF CONFIDENCE IS A SLAVE TO ELOQUENCE

And what is the reward for somebody who has found his voice? Self-confidence. The other day I came across a marvellous revelation of confidence, which you might call understandable conceit, from a barmaid: 'Life is easy for a girl if she is pretty and she can chat,' she said in a moment of sheer *joie de vivre*. Good on you sweetheart. The world was created for you.

Self-confidence is what we all seek. The horrible truth is it comes and goes throughout our lives, even from one situation to another during the same bloody day. Without this magic ingredient there can be no pleasure. I can give you a cast iron definition of self-confidence. It is quite simply knowing what to say next, which is what this book is all about. Conversely, fear is not knowing what to say next.

Journalist Elizabeth Mahoney interviewed television newscaster Sheena MacDonald, who had been suffering from memory deficiencies and language problems after being run over by a van. Referring to Sheena's husband, Mahoney wrote: 'After the accident, he took six months off to nurse her, spending the days working through crosswords, Scrabble, and word puzzles to improve her memory and language bank.'

Sheena explains to Mahoney that 'after a serious head injury, the part of the brain where language is stored gets so traumatised and paralysed that you can't find the words for the simplest things. I remember trying to find the word 'cashew' and could only come up with the word "gerbil".'

Mahoney comments: 'Only once in the interview does she lose her linguistic way, unable to recall what new projects she will be working on in coming months. Her face is a striking blend of panic and embarrassment, not an expression I ever thought I'd see in the once steely presenter.' She has had to join the rest of us. It is scary not being articulate.

It explains the terror so many people have about having to make a public speech. Incidentally, here is a tip from Bertie Wooster to his gormless friend Gussie Fink Nottle, who was daunted at the prospect of having to make a speech to a prep school: 'Cultivate a lofty contempt and pitch your voice to the fellow at the back.'

8 EVERYONE NEEDS A TURNIP

An artificial form of self-confidence comes from feeling superior to other people. We are only human. On first arrival at a party it is not unknown for a pretty woman to check for competition and get a rush of confidence if she discovers she is the *belle* no matter how small the ball, and a man loves it when he discovers he is the wittiest person in the room. Virginia Woolf notices this in *A Room of One's Own*: 'They say to themselves as they go into the room, I am the superior of half the people here, and it is thus they speak with their self confidence.'

This is how people near the top of the social pile can, over the years, come cascading down the slippery slope of other people's regard because such bolstering of one's ego is counter-productive. It can result in you avoiding the company of your social superiors who otherwise you could learn from and emulate. As the years go by, this can lead to a reduction of your social circle as you prioritise your desire to dominate other people rather than equate with them.

We all know chronic egotists – hollow versions of their former glory – who maybe have achieved positions of power in the world and surround themselves with lackeys, brown-noses and sycophants. It happens most noticeably in the world of work where talented people are overlooked in favour of the bosses' pets – people good at office politics – the ultimate art being how best to massage the bosses' ego while appearing to be merely conscientious.

Compare, compete and admire if necessary, but do not let it get you down. Do not let it reflect on you. Easier said than done because there do exist fantastic people whose DNA is right up there with the Gods. These beauticians of the human spirit are blessed with what I call the Chill Factor: Charm, Intelligence and Looks.

And yes, they can be frightening especially if you don't really know them and sometimes absolutely terrifying when you do because the Greeks were right: we are not born equal. They divided people into Gold, Silver and Bronze and inwardly we all know into which category we belong. I know I am Silver and I find myself adopting a different social attitude according to whom I am addressing. I am very different when I am talking to a Golden Figurine as opposed to a fellow Silver Salver or merely a Bronze Ornament.

I attempt to entertain the first. I am highly attentive to the second and I relax with the third. My friend Mark Hughes, who has married an intellectual high flyer and occasionally has to put up with academic house parties, says that he plays a very important role in these witty weekends. 'Everyone needs a turnip,' he says.

10 W. H. AUDEN IS ONE OF US

No, this isn't a book for those wonderful, happy, successful people who effortlessly get on well with other people and whose trials and tribulations are of other peoples' making.

'Good on you O *Jeunesse Doree*!' say I with every last trace of envy painstakingly erased from my conscious mind. 'Go out and enjoy your golden lives as much as you possibly can! Quite frankly, you owe it to the rest of us. If you come a cropper, it won't be your fault. Unwittingly, you will have married a bastard or a bitch or you will have been hit by ill health or, amazingly enough, considering all your advantages and your positive attitude to life, success will have eluded you in your chosen career.'

No, this is a book for the rest of us – people who find other people a problem. In any group there is an inner core who are having a great time. This is a book for the other, what I call periphery people, those of us who feel a couple of whiskies short of contentment. Some of us feel that beyond a few introductory remarks we have nothing to say, or even if we can gabble away like monkeys, beneath the veneer of sociability there yawns a terrible void. Some

of us feel that you have to be good at too many very often contradictory things in life and you have to muddle through as best you
can in a semi-incompetent state, flying along by the seat of your
pants. Some of us are becoming increasingly reduced in life to a
safe but dull routine of work, telly, bed. This does not impress
Shakespeare.

> What is a man,
> If his chief good and market of his time
> Be but to sleep and feed? A beast, no more.
> Sure he that made us with such large discourse,
> Looking before and after, gave us not
> That capability and god-like reason
> To fust in us unused.
>
> *Hamlet*, 4, 4

Are we just to seek various avenues of flight – drink, internet, drugs,
work and, if we are attractive enough, sex? Unfortunately, as we all
know, these coping strategies might provide temporary relief but
they are prey to the laws of diminishing returns.

'Socially for such a shy man the strain of conversation without his
Bennies could have been agonising. Without them he depended
instead far too heavily on alcohol.' Which verbally incompetent loser
does this quote from biographer Richard Davenport-Hines refer to
precisely? Only one of the most vocab-rich poets of the last century,
W. H. Auden!

CHAPTER SIX

Change

1 ARE YOU A LIFE TACKLER OR A CARPET SWEEPER?

The toughest amongst us are either soul searchers or pleasure seekers. Most of us, however, want a happy balance where our soul is fulfilled and pleasure is on tap. Then finally we can sit back and say, 'Yes, I am happy!' But it doesn't work like that because life is a continuous journey, spent in pursuit.

Love, for example, is most keenly felt in a spirit of yearning and you can only yearn for something when you have not got it. Not so long after it has been acquired, its intensity subsides into a gentler feeling of affection; after a longer period of time it becomes commonplace, taken for granted. Then, without you admitting to yourself, it can frequently dwindle into indifference.

Marital love is merely co-dependency, say the cynics. The only real love is a mother for her child, and to a lesser extent a father. Kids' love for their parents diminishes with age. Popular author Joanna Trollope says: 'Men love women. Women love children and children love hamsters.'

What do we really think? It depends if you are a believer or not. I am a believer. I believe in God, love, happiness, altruism, free-will and self-determination. I think they all exist, although access to them is difficult.

Yes, happiness is as slippery as a bar of soap, but that does not stop us obsessing about it even if we do not honestly think we will ever achieve it. Scientists are hilarious about the subject. They come up with their percentages, like the one already quoted about Scots being 40 per cent unhappier than the English. Don't you just love those dear solemn little psychologists, neurologists and biologists? Happiness, they say, is located in the left front cortex of the brain and depression happens when a thing called the amygdala is agitated in the right front cortex. 'Brains are things of habit and over time, each develops what researchers call a set point,' explains John Elliott in a *Sunday Times* article about the subject.

If your 'set point' is tilted to the left you will be blessed with a mind prone to feelings of happiness; if it is tilted to the right you will periodically fall victim to depression. 'Buddhists are gymnasts of the mind,' comments Elliott reporting on an eight week Buddhist immersion course designed to get the mind tilting to the left. The conclusion of his article was that you can train yourself to be happy. I agree with him. The technique is called prayer. But you try and do it! It's not easy. And it's very dull. In this book I am offering you a technique that is just as difficult, but much more entertaining. My recommended method is called making friends.

Anne Frank notes in her diaries that you have 'to earn your happiness'. I would add you must take steps to avoid unhappiness. Obviously there is nothing to be done about tragedy if you get ambushed by it. You have just got to take the hit. It's the gradual, seeping kind of unhappiness that requires your vigilance.

Beware all imitations. Freud says you can imitate happiness either by sublimation, which is the religious route (like Buddhists and their tilt to the left); deflection, which is the workaholics preferred approach; or desensitisation, a response favoured by the alcoholics, drug takers and sex addicts among us. Of course, most of us skirt around the happiness issue by adopting a mix of all three Freudian reactions. We distract ourselves by filling the day with a thousand tasks imposed on us by work and family. We dabble in religion, good works, politics, therapy, yoga, crystals or some other potty thing. And we are fond of a 'refreshment', as they say up here in the Highlands.

But the Freudian Dodge, as I call it, becomes increasingly less effective as we get older until we reach a point called the Mid-Life Crisis. Do we tackle life head on or do we sweep it under the carpet? The problem about being a Life Tackler is that you are in for an uncomfortable ride. The problem about Carpet Sweepers is that they condemn themselves to a gentle decline until they tip into an empty old age.

If you are not prepared to confront reality, you will end up with 'ego' on your face because it is your ego you must sacrifice in middle age if you want to leave adolescence. Most people die teenagers. Think of the number of old people you know who are not wise.

Change. That is what the Carpet Sweepers cannot bear to inflict on themselves. Actually the thing about change is you can't force it on yourself or, if you do, it will only be temporary. Change can only happen when you have arranged yourself so that there is no alternative. That normally involves trying out every other (less rigorous) option and by repetition being convinced of their failure.

2 SIX WAYS OF AVOIDING CHANGE

I am not saying change is easy. There are six obstacles, any one of which can get the better of you.

1. Time Misspent
2. Permanent Postponement
3. Mental Inertia
4. The Red Herring of Success
5. Low Morale
6. The Closed Mind

I have got a lovely story about time misspent, told to me by our parish priest. When I bumped into him the other day, he seemed to be amused and I asked him what he was smiling about. He said he had just come away from a conversation with an ex-parishioner of his who had explained to him why she no longer went to church.

'Oh father, there's just no time. The business has taken off and you know how it is. It's just spend, spend, spend!'

'And what do you spend your money on?' said the parish priest.

'Oh, perfume! I buy four or five different bottles a week and I get my sons to guess which one I've got on when I come down for breakfast in the morning.'

So her time is not totally misspent, I suppose, since at least it sounds like a fun start to the day!

A Course In Miracles is a wonderful thousand-page tome, anonymously written, giving you the wherewithal to perform a miraculous transformation in yourself. But its words of wisdom are wasted on you if you do not implement them. 'You are capable of enormous procrastination,' the book warns.

Our third obstacle is mental inertia. Sometimes we just can't be bothered to articulate a thought, come up with a reply or attend to the moment. We far prefer to switch on the television, take a drink, read a book, revert to an obsession, re-enter a daydream or tune into the car radio.

Worldly success can be a red herring, and the pursuit of it can distract us from more fundamental improvements that we might make in our lives. Real success is all about how you get on with your fellow man. All worldly success does is buy you entry into a different social environment. We had a classic case in our extended family where a chronically shy American with three university degrees and several million to his name, all of which he earned himself starting from naught, married a cousin of ours. Having finally got over feelings of shock, awe and amazement at the full extent of his reported wealth, people felt sorry for him because of his social ineptitude. At the end of the day we judge one another on social interaction.

Looking forward to adult life when I was a teenager, I did not think it was going to be a cake walk, but I had no idea it was virtually impossible. I never knew everything was going to be difficult: financially, intellectually, emotionally, socially, physically, culturally. Even something as natural as sex has turned out to be yet another bloody performance-related art form. Overcome with all these complications, life can feel like a fight to the death. There is a temptation to opt for the quiet life. Lift the carpet and start sweeping for all you are worth!

A marker of intelligence is the ability to change. It is one reason humans, not monkeys, are driving around in cars. By refusing to change you are making a monkey of yourself. Years ago I had the great pleasure of befriending Ted Hughes, who told me that most peoples' minds close half way through secondary school and that's them for life. They are set in one direction and all that happens is that they gain a certain expertise. Perhaps he is overstating the case, but I think we all know what he means. We see it all around us.

On the plus side, by middle age there is plenty of opportunity to change and plenty of reason. Gauguin's mid-life crisis was brought on by having been rejected by the woman he loved. This spurred him on to make critical decisions about his life. He found the nerve to jack in his job as a stockbroker and become a full time painter. Fear of poverty was nothing compared to the pain of romantic rejection.

It is easier to be bold if you feel you have got nothing to lose. There comes a point in your middle age, often brought on by some personal disaster or other, where your feel emboldened by your loss. Use that moment. It's golden. Teenagers are as bold as brass because they have got nothing to lose, but they cannot fully capitalise on that brilliant spirit of recklessness for lack of knowledge. The beauty of middle age is that you are finally in possession of the facts. You can redirect yourself away from the fantasy goals of adolescence.

A day without growth is a waste of a day and you have only got 10,000 of them in which to become the person you should be. That is the duration of your middle years, when you have enough life experience to be able to disentangle fact from fiction, and you still have enough life left to make it worth the effort.

And what is your reward? A rich old age. It's a hoot being old if you get it right. It was so sad Dylan Thomas never made it to old age, moaned his wife Caitlin, because he would have enjoyed it. He had fought the good fight, the battle for life, even if it was, as it always is, in an unconventional manner. His rewards would have come later after the day was done – in the evening.

3 ARE YOU IN CHARGE OF YOUR MIND?

What else should inspire you to grasp the nettle of change is to realise your own phenomenal potential. Proof of the untapped power of the mind I find in the instance of immortal tunes written and performed by teenagers, such as The Beatles or The Rolling Stones. Think of the explosion of pop music, its power, its grace, its brilliance and how it has conquered the world – all put together by a bunch of kids who have only just learnt to play their instruments. It just goes to show that where there is sufficient incentive, the mind does not hang about. You have just got to provide your own incentive.

'Compared with what we ought to be, we are only half awake. We are making use of only a small part of our physical and mental resources. Stating the thing broadly, the human individual thus lives far within his limits. He possesses powers of various sorts which he habitually fails to use,' writes US psychologist William James.

And what should you do with this amazing muscle called the mind? Get on top of it. Most people let their minds get on top of them with the result that they are at the mercy of its endless circular motion. Hence they are as predictable as yesterday's news and they are prone to obsession and repetition.

No, remember you are captain of your soul and master of your mind. You must consciously direct it in a way that you see fit. Your first job is to get into good self-enforced habits. This is an act of free will. Tell your mind to do it. Then one year, five years, ten years down the line you will discover that you are becoming, and then have become, the person created by those habits.

What is a job but an enforced habit, which is why salesmen all end up as salesmen even in their private lives. Some jobs are psychologically healthier than others.

At least if you are a lawyer you end up with good manners and a fine, if impersonal command of the English language. That is one of the points of prayer. If you pray an hour a day for a lifetime, grace gathers about your person – you get a good feel about you. Conversely bad habits take their toll. So promiscuous people end up looking seedy. Manipulative people start to look hard. Fake people, like adulterers, thieves and conmen, are more difficult to spot because they are actively projecting reverse images of themselves. From twenty years of employing people for work in pubs and restaurants, where pilfering is a major issue, I have learnt that nobody looks dishonest but dishonest people do not actively look honest. What feed your aura are your habits.

4   ARE YOU A REAL MAN OR A PLAYBOY?

What it boils down to is this – are you a real man or a playboy? Real men chat. Playboys make conversation. Real men are themselves. Playboys act themselves. Real men are absolute. Playboys are relative. Real men do the marathon. Playboys are sprinters. Real men are quietly spoken. Playboys exaggerate. Real men can play. Playboys playact. Real men are independent. Playboys copy. Real men are grounded. Playboys are immaterial. Real men laugh at what other people say. Playboys laugh at what they say themselves.

Have you ever noticed how so many people laugh at their own jokes? They tell a joke or funny story then they roar with laughter. Presumably they already know the punch line, so why are they laughing? It is pure ego massage, self-pleasing, a taking delight in self. A real man is delighted with other people when they surprise him with something amusing. He loves the shock of the unknown or unexpected given a humorous twist. There are four responses to the mid-life challenge:

1. Give up and become a work, telly, bed recluse.
2. Keep recovering from failure and re-entering the fray, only to be knocked back again.
3. Form set-piece coping mechanisms and self-defence strategies.
4. Analyse, implement and persist.

Real men and women opt for number four, the way of this book. The analysis is horribly simple. Mid-life crisis is that point in your life when you realise not only that you are not the person you thought you were, but also you have failed to become the person you should be. At this critical point you should then try and shed the artificial projection of your self and also embrace your reality.

Learning to share conversation and make real friends is the most effective method of discovering yourself or, in a lot of instances, rediscovering yourself. Very often you were more fully yourself at school or university, both genuine communities highly conducive to the nourishment of the human spirit, than in subsequent years when you have had to fight a lone battle for financial survival in a comparatively hostile environment.

5 TALK REVOLUTION IS THE SOLUTION

The way back and forward is through words. The first part of this book is about analysis. The second part is about implementation: how to gain command of your own unique way of speaking and what daily exercises you need to do to bring about that mastery. Persisting is an exercise of will on your part. Motivation you have to provide for yourself in the form of reminders of purpose and signs of progress.

A self-help book has to analyse a particular problem, offer a persuasive solution, and then devise a program of exercises that can turn theory into actuality. The problem here is alienation. The solution is communion. The exercise is talk.

6 TALK IS NOT NATURAL. IT IS AN ART FORM.

The problem with words in their spoken form is the widespread belief that talking is natural. You just open your mouth and out come the words. It is, of course, as much an art form as writing, only more difficult because you are given such little time in which to reply. Talking is like writing on speed. No wonder it is such a haphazard affair and so many people are not very good at it.

What is incredible is our whole happiness is dependent on this art form and yet we don't study it. Our schools are scandalously remiss. We are taught History (how to rule a country), Geography (where that country is), Science (what everything is), Maths (how to count), English (how to read a book) and French (how to murder a foreign language).

Of course, it didn't used to be like that. Up until the last world war, public school education used to be concerned solely with use of language. It was called a classical education because you studied the classics. All you learnt was Latin and Greek, dull as ditch water but it taught you through the driest means possible the nuts and bolts of the English language.

These boys basically spent the entire decade of their school years painstakingly translating Latin and Greek into English, word by gruesome word, and back again. In the process language was analysed for them and they got to master its vocabulary, syntax and composition. In those days language was the point of education.

'All the Elizabethan dramatists were formed by their grammar school training which was intensely and solely verbal, focused on reading, analysing and reproducing literary forms. Shakespeare learnt everything from his schooling, life-long reading and observation of life,' writes the reviewer Richard Woods.

Churchill was slow in all subjects except English, so he remained in the same class 'three times longer than anyone else' with a master who specialised in teaching 'stupid' boys to write English. As a result Churchill says he developed a love of English.

'Naturally I am biased in favour of boys learning English. I would make them all learn English: and then I would let the clever ones learn Latin as an honour and Greek as a treat. But the only thing I would whip them for not knowing is English. I would whip them hard for that,' wrote Churchill.

People of my father's generation stepped out of school with total command of the language. They would shudder at the slightest linguistic infelicity. Of course we still have English Language class today, but it's nothing in comparison to the depth and breadth of what my father's generation were taught. The ancient Greeks went one step further. One of the prime subjects at their schools was rhetoric. Even education in the Communist Soviet Union had a greater respect for language. Eugenie Vronskaya, my Russian émigré neighbour, said that at school in Moscow they not only had rhetoric class, they also used to have to memorise poetry and act out scenes from literature. The values most prized in the Islamic culture are generosity, courage, appreciation of nature and, interestingly, poetry and eloquence.

Not learning a proper use of language at school is as shambolic as training for football without the use of a ball. Ex-England manager Bobby Robson can recall the 1950s when football coaching was in its infancy and as a result the standard of football was pitiful compared to today's amazing play. It used to consist of charging down the wing and punting the ball across to the centre for a forward to head in to the net, or else hoofing the ball up the middle of the park in the hope that somebody got a lucky bounce. 'Preparation for a First Division match consisted of 5, 4, 3, 2, 1 – run 5 laps, walk 1, run 4, walk 1 and so on. We'd ask: 'Can we have a ball for training?' And the reply would come: 'What do you want a ball for? You'll get one on Saturday.' That was the way it was for every club,' says Bobby Robson.

Preparation is everything in art as well as sport. Talent is merely attitude. Facility is speed. The rest is slog. The artist Matisse used to amaze the world with the way he could knock off a nude in under a minute. The secret of his incredible skill was Presbyterian self-discipline at the outset of his career. With ruler, compass and graph paper he would precisely measure the exact outline of a nude to scale. Then he would trace that line for days and days until he could get the dimensions spot on at any given point, then he merely accelerated the process until he had got the whole job down to a minute.

This is an important method of education. It is basically the PHD principle. Specific concentration on any given subject to the nth degree will train your mind to scale the heights. Tony Benn is one of the greatest contemporary public speakers, tosh though the content might be. He was not born an orator. He became one through gruesome preparation. At the Oxford Union he used to set aside one hour of preparation for every minute of public speech. Now, of course, public speaking has become second nature to him and he can think on his feet. But that was how he gained his mastery.

So to recap: the aim of life is happiness, which depends on how we get on with other people. Assuming you are basically a decent person, this depends not so much on the extent of your virtue but on the quality of your conversation. And because conversation is an art form, this depends on the effectiveness of your preparation and the power of your concentration.

7   GENERAL KNOWLEDGE IS MERELY DISTRACTION. MAKE IT PARTICULAR.

The whole of religion is based on the notion of preparation, and so is education. In one context the medium is prayer and in the other it's learning. Most people suffer from limited learning systems because they are controlled by their scripts. That is they put themselves first, which is a mix of social and cultural conditioning inherited from their family-background and picked from their contemporary environment. So most people only learn among pre-set trajectories. They do not start like philosophers, who take great pains first to disassociate themselves before embarking on a course of study. A philosopher says you can take nothing for granted. He views the subject solely according to its merits. First remove the ego, then immerse yourself in the subject.

There are two basic levels of learning: first changing errors within a framework of beliefs and values, then secondly changing the actual framework. What I have been trying to do so far in this book is persuade you, the reader, of the need to go through this rigorous regime. Learning is all about acquiring knowledge – the purpose of information, the reason you go out and gather the stuff, the data. So you only learn something if there is a point to it. For example, I think there is a fortune to be made out of raspberry jam. There is not a raspberry jam on the market with the colour, bouquet and taste of a genuine home-made raspberry jam that you can buy at a church fete. And to me raspberry jam is the best tasting jam in the world. This has made me track down the top WRI jam maker in the parish and listen attentively to how she goes about making her jam. What she said to me was simple but fascinating because, although she did not realise it, she was giving me the secret recipe to a fortune.

This woman was my fortune cookie. She told me the key to jam is not to boil it to death and to avoid artificial setting agents even if you have to sacrifice a little on consistency. Industrial jam manu-facturers make a God out of firmness and so muck up the purity of the taste with gelatine and boil away the goodness of the jam. My departure from convention is to side with the housewife and allow a certain sloppiness.

Twenty years as a small time entrepreneur has made me realise that overheads, primarily in the form of property and equipment, gobble up profit. So I have started a company called 101 Housewives where I get the housewives to make raspberry jam themselves. They cook on their cookers, in their own kitchens, using their gas or electricity, but they do it according to my sloppy recipe using my ingredients in my labelled pots. I call the jam home made, stick an extra 80p premium on the price for the privilege and give it to the housewife. I get the profit: QED, A1 GP, ASAP for KF and no VAT!

8 FOUR STYLES OF LEARNING

There are four styles of learning:

1. An active learner is someone who sees the point of information as how it affects what he does. It is in doing something that he learns about the activity. That is the person who wants to know how actually to make the jam.
2. A pragmatist is somebody who needs to know the practical relevance of what he is being asked to learn. Before being interested in all the detail of jam making, he needs to know how it is going to make him money.
3. A reflector is a philosopher. For him, experience precedes knowledge. He takes part in the entire jam making project and then reflects on the experience in all its myriad implications.
4. A theorist is an academic. He sees the patterns that underwrites data, the laws that govern behaviour. He is the person who came up with the idea of how and why there was a fortune to be made out of the mass production through individual means of sloppy home-made raspberry jam.

9 KNOWLEDGE IS UNDERSTANDING, NOT FACT FINDING

Knowledge is not a question of stockpiling information. Somebody without any academic qualification at all can be, and often is, more knowledgeable than somebody with a string of letters after his name. There is an interesting exchange in the film *Billy Elliot* between a middle class boy and our working class hero, Billy, at the Royal Ballet School where they meet waiting to be interviewed for admission.

'Where do you come from?'
'Durham.'
'Durham? Isn't there an amazing cathedral?'
'I don't know.'

What we see here is a culture clash. It appears that the middle class boy is showing up the working class boy's staggering ignorance about his home town but, in fact, the middle class boy is lacking knowledge at a much deeper level. He is unaware of the value of silence. He has been socially conditioned to be forward. The emphasis in his background is to train him for management, for him to be assertive, to dominate, compete and win. His private education has provided him with many more items of general information: ultimately meaningless, a sort of Trivial Pursuit attitude to knowledge. What is the point of a boy knowing that Durham has an amazing cathedral when what he doesn't know is how to get on with somebody of his own age from that city – with the result, incidentally, that he ends up being punched to the ground for his impertinence.

Real knowledge is about understanding how to deal with the huge variety of human being in this world. It is much more important that Billy Elliot knows how to get on with all sorts of different people in Durham than the fact there is a marvellous cathedral in town. He is concentrating on the right stuff. He is like people who know the name of the postman but not the name of the Chancellor of the Exchequer. Obviously that is the right set of priorities. You are never going to meet the Chancellor of the Exchequer whereas you come across the postman every day.

CHAPTER SEVEN

Listen

1 THE MOST DIFFICULT INSTRUMENT IN THE ORCHESTRA IS THE SECOND FIDDLE

The art of conversation is to listen to the other person and respond to what he or she says, using your own material to fill in the gaps if necessary. Often people are not very good at the little things, like laughing and listening. They feel they have got to fight their corner, especially in this modern world where community has been decimated, employment carries no security and people are described in terms of mobility of labour and staffing issues.

In the free market of capitalism, people are not only sold. You also have to sell yourself to prove that you are better than your fellow man. This does not make for an environment where you encourage or appreciate your neighbour. Instead of enjoying his story, you find yourself wracking your brain thinking of ways in which you can cap it with a better one of your own.

I am not singling out men earning a living in the cutthroat corporate world as being particular offenders. In my experience, creative people tend to be even worse. Often they try to be brilliant all the bloody time, which is exhausting not only for themselves but for everybody else as well. The other problem is they can get locked into themselves as one verbal gem triggers another in a seemingly endless ingenious sequence.

Being a poet you would have thought Yeats would be a sensitive man possessing empathy for the needs of others, yet he admitted of himself: 'I do not listen enough. It is not merely that I talk, for if I were in a silent room, I still do not really listen. A word suggests something and I follow that. I am always like a child playing with bricks in the corner.' There you have it – the basic autism at the heart of all genius. Talent can make you more interested in yourself than other people. You simply do not know what you are going to say next.

There was an interesting moment in the 2001 Comic Relief Celebrity Big Brother series when comedian Jack Dee and TV presenter Vanessa Feltz both admitted to one another they found each another difficult to talk to. He said that her problem was that she did not seem real: she was all projection, no content. She said she felt he was an oppressive presence.

I would not say either of them look like easy company, and that is the goal of society. It is the ultimate social compliment. It means a person is human, relaxed, sympathetic, attentive, responsive. These are not the qualities of great performers and, of course, Jack Dee and Vanessa Feltz earn their living through performance. It was a fascinating moment where we got behind the mask of the clown. Oh the limitations of somebody who always needs to be the centre of attention, no matter how brilliant!

The most difficult instrument in the orchestra is the second fiddle. Think on those heroic spouses and partners who have married above their station and are condemned to a life in the shadows. Think of Dennis Thatcher, Ernie Wise and a million long suffering women sacrificed on the altar of their husband's ego. The four spiritual strengths listed in the vocational book *Spiritual Practices* are tenderness, perception, appreciation and humility – all qualities required of a good listener. Humility especially is needed for people condemned to play the second fiddle.

2 WHAT IS THE ULTIMATE TEST OF A GOOD LISTENER?

The litmus test that distinguishes great listeners from good ones is the ability to concentrate on an ordinary conversation when bang next door to you, well within earshot, is a riveting person entertaining the socks off a delighted woman. People with such powers of concentration do exist and they invariably have unbelievable charisma. I know two such people, one of each sex, within my social circle. They possess a marvellous absolutism. Their attention to you is exclusive.

My teenage niece, Caroline, had the incredible privilege of meeting President Clinton at a social gathering in New York. I asked her how his charisma had affected her. She said that what he does is listen to every word you say as if you were more important than him. You can see what Caroline means if you watch the film *Primary Colours* with John Travolta giving a very personable imitation of Bill Clinton.

3   YOU CAN ONLY TALK AS WELL AS THE OTHER PERSON LISTENS

Some people are boring. Other people make those around seem boring. Have you ever been tongue-tied in front of somebody with a reputation as a social star? The fault can either lie with you or them. Another's brilliance can strike fear or joy in your heart depending on how competitive you are. You are to blame for your silent envy. But there are others who take all the oxygen out of the air, rendering their acquaintances speechless. Here is a golden rule. You can only talk as well as the other person listens.

The better the listener, the better the *craic*. The seminal play *Waiting for Godot* is all about two men who do not listen to one another. It is the stereotypical male conversation consisting of what John O'Donohue calls 'parallel monologues'. Beckett illustrates that ultimately we are all alone and nobody ever really connects with anyone else. His play suited the climate of the times but we don't have to be fashionably cynical. We all (rather boringly) know that love and friendship do exist. As O'Donohue rightly says: 'Communication is salvation.'

I myself am a terrible culprit. I hoover up attention, show off as if life was a circus, and use both ears for listening: the left one for the conversation I am having and the right one for the one I am not having. Half the time it's as if I were deaf. I have noticed myself inadvertently repeat a question not because the other person has failed to answer it to my satisfaction but because I have been so uninterested I have failed to remember what I asked in the first place.

4   SUCCESS IS HEARD

However, in business, where my livelihood is dependent on information, I listen like the aural equivalent of a hawk. In business, unlike in my social life, I let other people do the talking. I ply them with questions – really relevant questions, and I am curious about the reply. I even have the patience to listen to masses of stuff I already know and a lot of bullshit that I have long since discarded, in the off chance that I will learn something I don't know, some little insight, a piece of information that will help grow my business. All I do in business is apply maths, logic and intuition to the information I harvest from other people.

> The humble bumble businessman
> One Two Three Four Five
> The humble bumble businessman
> Keeps us all alive.

You can search the length and breadth of literature and you will not find a sympathetic portrait of a businessman – yet look what happened to the communist world when they tried to do without these well-mannered and besuited intermediaries between capital and labour. They are the ultimate listeners and talkers. Great business people are also good talkers because they not only need sound judgment, but they have to persuade other people of their convictions.

My father had sound judgment and was a great listener, but he did not have the professional jargon necessary to operate successfully at senior corporate level. When he sold his poultry business to a big animal foodstuffs conglomerate, and he joined their board of directors, he found that the directors' decisions went against his better judgment with adverse effects on the company. He forfeited authority through lack of familiarity with corporate language, so no one really listened to what he was saying.

5   HOW TO BE COOL

More than half of listening is done with our eyes. According to a recent research study, 55 per cent of communication between people is carried out though body language; only 7 per cent is transmitted through actual words. The rest of chat is divided into what they call tone, pace and mode of delivery. What they are saying is that when two people are having a furious row, they are so mesmerised by their mutual anger that the words exchanged are almost superfluous. At the other end of the emotional spectrum you have lovers whispering sweet nothings. Literally it does not matter what they are saying because what they are really telling one another in a million different ways are the three words that offer the passport to the heaven of romance.

The important point to be deduced from this is that it is style, not content that matters in conversation. You will notice that although really popular people seem always to be engaged in animated conversation at social gatherings, very often the content of what they are saying can be surprisingly ordinary.

Conversational style, as the studies show, is not just verbal dexterity, it is mostly manner and rhythm. Adolescents experiment with a variety of conversational styles before they eventually settle on what works best for them, which tends to be a combination or variation on what they have inherited from their parents.

Youth mania for cool is entirely justified because it recognises that social success is 93 per cent determined by style. The question is not whether you are a good or bad person, but whether you are good or bad company. There are some people who might be fascinating, if only you could be bothered to concentrate on what they were saying. But their mode of delivery is too dry to make it worth the effort. You would be far happier reading what they had to say and dispensing with the physical presence altogether.

6 SPEAK AT THE SPEED OF YOUR HEART

Rhythm comes from your soul and the problem with so many of us is that we are out of tune with ourselves. You should never speak faster than your heart beats. Only talk at speed when you are angry – that way you quicken the duration of your anger. We are quite rightly suspicious of fast talkers. We feel they whizz quickly over the surface of a subject because no particular point bears scrutiny. They don't explore a subject in our company. What we are getting is a ready-cooked meal of opinion reheated. Often it is non-thinking, pre-recorded people, like salesmen, who talk at speed.

People accelerate their rhythm of speech when they are frightened, such as when they first arrive at a party, when they are lying, or when they are telling a joke. Many a good joke has been lost to stage fright. I am incredibly attentive to other people's jokes and am relieved when they are funny, but I am always careful not to laugh too much in case the fellow tries another one on me.

7 FUNNY IS NOT WHAT BUT HOW

The really funny people, as opposed to those of us who are merely witty, are funny not because of what they say so much as the way they say it. Stand up comedian Frank Carson's famous catchphrase was 'It's the way I tell them!' and he was right. Lack of rhythm gives comics the blues.

What gives you rhythm? Anything that connects you with yourself, other people, or God. So sport, yoga, prayer, physical and creative work, conversation, love and drink give you rhythm. Television, administration, sales, drugs, money, fantasy, desire and drink take away your rhythm. Yes, drink gives and takes away your rhythm. Drink feels like home. It is only the next day you realise it was rented accommodation. As Homer Simpson says: 'Drink is the problem and the solution.'

As we all know, life is a journey. You are the driver and the car is your mind. You should change gear according to the social situation. In your dealings with people you want to get to fourth gear as quickly as possible. The problem is some people get stuck in first gear and they are exhausting to be with. You get other people with real self possession and they have a beautiful natural rhythm – a low purring charisma. Whatever they say sounds compelling.

Having said all that, the reason why the 7 per cent (the actual words) are more important than the other 93 per cent (that is the body language, tone, pace and mode of delivery) is that, as I have pointed out earlier, the definition of self-confidence is knowing what to say next and it is self-confidence that determines the other four elements of the communication pie chart. A more interesting way round the problem is to get the other person to do the talking. For that you have to develop your curiosity.

8   SEVEN WAYS TO REPLY

The proof of how well you are listening to somebody is to be found in how accurately you respond to them, when it comes to your turn to talk. There are seven ways to reply to somebody.

1. Relating an experience of your own that refers to the subject being discussed or story told.
2. Saying what the other person is saying, but in a different way.
3. Disagreeing with reasons, provoking a discussion.
4. Offering sympathy: tapping into feeling with comment.
5. Developing the other person's story or argument.
6. Asking a supplementary question.
7. Laughing.

Real laughter never fails. It relaxes everybody and almost

immediately makes the other person, who is getting the automatic endorphin attendant on applause, try to repeat the experience. Laboratory rats prove that.

Questions are also a good stand-by if all else fails. It is perfectly acceptable in society to ask a dozen questions in a row especially now that a lot of conversations we witness come in the form of television interviews. The value of questions is that they open up the other person and they allow you to broaden the scope of the topic under review. In the introductory stages of conversation I am invariably struck by how great socialites often ply you with questions until they find something that interests them, which they latch on to and develop into a fanciful conceit or interesting discussion.

CHAPTER EIGHT

Identity

1 WHAT TYPE OF PERSON ARE YOU?

You must factor your own character into the equation. Are you an optimist or a pessimist? An idealist or a sceptic? A fantasist or a cynic? You cannot be both a cynic and a fantasist, but an idealist can be a realist with ideas. Wannabes tend to be fantasists. *Wanna-havebeens*, like critics, tend to be cynics. And there is no satisfying a cynic, just like there is no pleasing a football fan except momentarily during the orgasm of a goal because a minute later they are back in negative mode.

The social default position of the British is either quick-fire sarcasm, total scepticism or knowing whimsy. Theatre director Peter Hall draws attention to the former reaction when he describes the conversational style of Britain's ruling elite. He writes of 'the jocular ruthlessness which characterises the establishment on a night out.' Look no further than P. G. Wodehouse for the ultimate comedy style of a believer.

2 THE PERCEPTION MATRIX

One word of caution is that you may not be correct in evaluating your own character. To find out who you are, you need to draw up what I call a 'perception matrix' consisting of four boxes. You need to compile observations about yourself from your spouse, your friends, your enemies and yourself. Those four sets of opinions normally give a pretty complete picture of a person.

Fantasists think they are idealists and cynics think they are realists. I used to think I was an optimist, but when I discovered that I had been betrayed by my wife I was intrigued by my lack of surprise, thus discovering how deeply cynical I must really have been. Of course, humour is to do with affection; where relations are not cordial, the tone starts to go wrong and so, for example, the mock abuse of a cynic can be a little heavy on the abuse side of things.

3 MORE IS LESS

One way of finding out what type of person you really are is by analysing how you talk. Certain styles of talk suit certain styles of thinking and you will naturally adopt the manner and tone of your real belief system. The celebrated literary critic Cyril Connolly, author of *Enemies Of Promise*, divided literary styles into Mandarin and colloquial. He made the fascinating observation that believers were full of purpose and so their writing style tended to be plainer (colloquial) because they were trying to get across a message. They set a premium on communication with the reader. Nonbelievers, on the other hand, were more interested in entertainment and so their literary style was ornate.

If you do not believe in anything, life can only be a game. Amongst the nonbelievers you get great entertainers like Oscar Wilde, Byron and the Amises – but woe betide members of this crew who try and get serious, like that fleet of incomprehensible poets starting with T. S. Eliot and their counterparts in fiction like Sartre, Gide and a lot of second rate copycats including that egg-headed woman, not Virginia Woolf but the other one, A. L. Somebodyorother.

Of course, the vast majority of writers are believers because they have seen the other side. Nihilistic movements like 'punk' are fun for shock value and an exclamation of outrage, but they are a thing of youth. Ultimately they don't get you anywhere. So writers of that persuasion can make an early splash and subsequent works have to depend totally on style for their effect. Will Self is a classic case: a person of huge literary promise unfulfilled – a sad case of arrested development. He got stuck up his own arse in his adolescence and has failed to climb out. I am not surprised disbelief stunts literary growth. But worse than nonbelievers are fake believers like Iris Bloody Murdoch. God she's boring!

4   WHAT IS YOUR NATURAL HABITAT?

The next thing you need to realise is your own natural comfort zone. You need to work hard on areas of social engagement that are foreign to your style of personality. Ask yourself whether you are naturally more comfortable in an intimate situation where it is just two people in conversation or whether you prefer, as a lot of teenagers do, to be in a social group or a small gang of friends (a private situation), or indeed the relative anonymity of a party: the public domain. Communication in the universal dimension is to do with self expression in the form of religion, politics, philosophy and the arts.

People behave and so talk very differently in these four different environments. To be a full, rounded person, to get the most out of life, you need to be proficient and therefore comfortable in all four situations. You can enjoy being with somebody at category one, what the French call a *tête à tête*, eschew them at category two as maybe they suffer from an inability to relax in a group on account of wanting too much personal attention, attach yourself to them at category three because they are good fun at a party, and be pleasantly surprised by them at category four when you discover they are capable of knocking out a passable poem.

5   HOW TO COPE WITH THE THREE LEVELS OF SOCIETY

The problem with listening is that people prefer to talk. When you talk well, you immediately get that feeling of air to the ego. Ideally one would like to keep the fellow fully inflated at all times. However, in this cruel world where other people exist, they need to feel good as well. This involves having to listen to them. And, as discussed earlier, people perform at three different levels. They are either better than you, worse then you or as good as you. Coming from class-ridden Britain we are very familiar with this grading system: upper, lower, middle. Indeed we even have a class called best. Aristos is Greek for best.

But in the real world we judge one another according to how well we speak. Jimmy Reid, the Glasgow shipyard trade union leader, was quoted in the *Sunday Times* as saying: 'It is ironic, but the well-heeled are seldom a bundle of laughs. The hard up are.' The problem is how to cope with your social superiors and by that phrase, as you will now have gathered, I mean people who operate in a socially superior way to you. One tip is to realise that very often people do not feel as good as they look, which is reassuring.

One way of putting yourself on an equal footing with your social superiors is to get them out of their natural habitat. If somebody is great at a party, try and get him or her alone in a car journey. A universalist, such as a brilliant professor or an incredible actor, might dominate an audience of hundreds and yet wilt around a kitchen table. Universalists are famous for their comparative social incompetence because they spend too long by themselves. I love reviewer Celia Brayfield's description of writers as possessing 'toxic jealousy, crap social skills and poor personal hygiene.'

All we try and do is find the human being in one another, which means uncovering one another's weaknesses so that we can relax sufficiently to appreciate one another's strengths. Of course, with social inferiors, you have got to hunt for what is worth while in them. Get them on their territory and metaphorically tickle them under the arms. Everybody responds to affectionate teasing.

Drink also makes other people appear to be more interesting. It also very helpfully serves to lower your own critical standards. Never forget the importance of people lower down the social hierarchy than yourself. Remember they make you feel good. Have you ever been to a social gathering where everyone is an 'A' lister? It's a nightmare. People hardly dare say anything for fear of not being fascinating.

The epitome of drawing room wit and erudition in the history of English society was the literary social circle known as the Bloomsbury Group with the *avant garde* novelist Virginia Woolf as its prime hostess. What a relief, she says, when you get to know somebody well enough and finally there is 'no need to hurry, no need to sparkle, no need to be anybody but oneself.' So even she was daunted by other people's brilliance.

I also recommend scapegoats as a way of relieving tension amongst a group of obviously marvellous people. A scapegoat unites a group and puts you in with the majority unless, of course, you happen to be the one singled out for the honour of spreading peace and good-will amongst your peers. Scape-goatery is quite a bonding experience and gives everybody a nice warm glow of comradeship and, more importantly, a socially acceptable excuse to be nasty, which can be a huge relief from the superhuman effort of having to be nice all the time.

That leaves people of your own standard. You should try and make friends with them. Always suspect anybody who tags on after their social superiors or surrounds themselves with their inferiors. Complexes are at work and they are not being combated.

My favourite image to describe this business of having to talk above, below and beside yourself is the seating arrangements in a car. If I am talking to somebody superior to me, it feels as if I am travelling in the back seat of the car. If I am talking to somebody of my own worth, I imagine I am sitting in the front passenger seat and if I am with my social inferior, I am in the driving seat. We pretend to be egalitarian but we know its nonsense. Ten minutes in the outside world teaches us that. There are geniuses and duffers – and then there is you.

So now you start to appreciate the hideous complexity of being a fully socially integrated human being. You have to be competent in twelve different social situations, for example you might have to be able to handle a dimwit in a universal category of exchange or you may have to cater for your social equal in a situation that is too intimate, like a hotel lift, or you might have to deal with your social superior taking too much of an interest in your wife at a party.

No matter what the situation, the golden rule about being British is you have to maintain a permanent air of friendliness. It is this very fact that recommended Austria to the celebrated humorist and journalist A. A. Gill when he wrote that the great thing about Austria was its anonymity and its formality. The people in Austria do not do small talk, he says: 'Watching the Viennese go about their daily business, you see they're not people people; not particularly warm to each other. What they are instead is polite, with immensely good, lightly starched manners, and this is such a joy after coming from a social climate of enforced, instant mateyness and small talk. The thoughtful formality of etiquette is a blessed relief. You forget what a strain friendliness is until you don't have it.'

6 HOW TO TALK TO SOMEONE OF THE OPPOSITE SEX

Communication is further complicated by the fact that human beings come in two shapes: male and female. The science of evolution teaches us that a man wants a woman who will be a good breeder, so the physique is important, and a women wants a man who is a good provider, so the wallet is important. A man would never say: 'I really fancy my boss. She's not really good looking as such, but she's got a brilliant sense of humour and, OK, she's got a bit of a beer belly but what a lovely smile!'

Woman love men they admire. Men love women they worship. The poet William Blake described the naked female form as 'a portion of eternity too great for the eye of man'. You would not say that about the body of a man. Visually, we just can't compete.

Kingsley Amis said about women's breasts: 'Before I ever had dealings with any breast, I knew I would like them, I never knew how much I would like them.' You would never hear a woman raving about balls. They might say something stupid like 'O I feel so safe in his strong arms!', which is merely another expression of admiration.

Now you understand why men have to show off to women and women have to wear make-up. Feminism may have transformed the lot of women, or many of them, but much of it is wishful thinking like, for example, people of the opposite sex genuinely being friends. You go to the pub with a mate. She just happens to be a stunning beauty. Why is your wife making such a racket with the pots and pans?

Genitals affect the way we talk to one another. Man always have an ulterior motive lurking, even if it is in their subconscious. That is the way we are programmed. Sex plays havoc with conversation. It can turn perfectly sensible men into buffoons and perfectly capable women into simpering idiots. Women, of course, retain the right of veto, but even if a woman doesn't fancy you she'll probably want you to fancy her.

It is in fact considered the height of bad manners not to pretend to a woman that, but for a million obstacles, you would have sex with her. Otherwise it assumes she is not attractive; as Shakespeare so rightly says: 'Woman, thy name is vanity.'

I wrote a poem on the subject once. A woman had invited me to a supper as a friend. In the course of the evening she knocked back all my advances, insisting we keep our relationship on the basis of friendship. It was only when I was finally about to get in my car, persuaded by her arguments, that she treated me to an unexpected amorous embrace. She hadn't suddenly started to fancy me or anything, but she certainly did not want me to stop fancying her.

On her own terms

'No,' she said. 'No, I told you not to touch.'
Nor was I allowed a lighted candle
Between us for fear of causing scandal.
Would she care to share my salad? Not much.

The offer of a massage was refused.
A suggested trip to Paris was banned.
And kissing was forbidden out of hand.
Any talk of sex? She was not amused.
Of all the crimes there's one she won't forgive.
You can gaze upon her face, her eyes, her nose and lips
But woe betide your eyes that rest upon her tits.
Better not to love. Better not to live.
And yet because it is her female right
She disobeyed herself in the moonlight.

There is a lovely line in *Brideshead Revisited* when Charles Ryder lights a cigarette for Julia Flyte and hands it over from his lips to hers while she is driving and he feels 'a bat squeak of desire'. I maintain that there is always 'a bat squeak of desire' present in conversation between a man and a woman and so there is invariably an undercurrent of the courtship ritual at play.

Conversely talk between heterosexual men is based on physical revulsion. There is anti-magnetism at work, which explains how inter-male talk is primarily abusive, no matter how leavened by humour or sublimated by ideal. Women, on the other hand, are not physically revolted by one another, so their talk is more intimate.

Evolutionarily speaking, Men must have had a lot less time or need for conversation than women. You don't need to speak much to be an effective hunter. There would be no food and probably no sex if you came back from your hunting trip describing the nuanced emotions involved in not-quite catching a mammoth. If there was a problem, you needed to solve it, not talk about it. Even to this day women are not impressed by the man who witters on about his problems. She wants the man who has solved them so she can enjoy the fruits of his success.

Nobody is all man or all women. We are just predominantly one or the other. Possibly one of the advantages of being an only son in a family of women would be exposure at the language forming age of childhood to female conversational habits. You could attribute Bill Clinton's phenomenal powers of empathy in general, and success with women in particular, to just such a childhood. He was a lone male child surrounded by women. The result was a magical mix: the multi-tasking, million worded, caring, sharing, intuitive, mendacious alpha male – a consummate politician.

No wonder in his two terms of office, despite any amount of scandal, he somehow retained the affection, if not the approval, of most of his electorate. Margaret Thatcher was the opposite. Like many effective decision-makers, she expressed complex thoughts in as few words as possible. My uncle once had to give a presentation to Thatcher and he was advised to put all his findings on one side of an A4. There was not a problem in the world, according to Mrs Thatcher, that could not be summarised on one side of an A4 piece of paper in such a way as to enable a solution.

7 THE LESS YOU DO THE MORE YOU TALK

St Paul was the ultimate man of action. His job was to save the world by converting it to Christianity and he succeeded. Without the use of modern communication he had to advertise Christ's sacrifice. How did he do it? Was it with breath-taking eloquence? Was it with unanswerable scholarship? No, it was, as he said in his letter to the Corinthians, with 'great plainness of speech'. When there is a serious job to be done, you keep it simple. On television Maggie Thatcher used to speak to us like we were at primary school.

8 TO DO OR TO BE

You are either a *do-er* or a *be-er*. A wordsmith or an action man, or ideally but quite rarely, a happy combination. Incidentally, I do not prioritise *do-ers* over *be-ers*, if anything the reverse. Highly developed people don't actually do anything. Management gets other people to implement their commands and, of course, truly

advanced *be-ers* can't even manage. Here I am thinking of soph-
isticates, philosophers, mystics, socialites and academics –
supposedly the cream of society.

You could almost say action men do stuff because they can't
talk. It accords with the compensation theory of human behaviour.
Doing covers for lack of being. In this instance action compensates
for lack of conversation, an expression of being. Action men let
money and status, the fruits of their action, do their talking.

Wordsmiths are generally hopeless at action. Committees are run
by wordsmiths. There is no place in a committee for an action
man. They turn their collective nose up at him. He is far too crude,
rude, impatient and impetuous and he in turn gets frustrated with
them. Action men are sole traders and freelance operators. They
are eschewed by the system. The only place for them is either by
themselves or at the very top.

Basically, our country and all its institutions are run by
wordsmiths – but words have a terrible way of running away with
you, especially in the mouths and pens of legislators and bureaucrats.
Words can be little dictators when they are created in a vacuum.
We have all got crazy bureaucratic stories from the Health and Safety
department. I read the other day of an avenue of chestnut trees in
Norfolk that had to be cut down for fear of the conkers falling on
the heads of children. My music venue was visited by a pair of
Health and Safety officials who ordered me to put a banister up the
two steps leading to the stage. I tried to point out that if somebody
actually missed their footing, they would fall only the full fourteen
inches, and incidentally we were currently bombing the bejesus out
of the Iraqis. A little perspective I was calling for, but not getting.

. . .

CHAPTER NINE

Talk

1 THE SIX TOPICS OF TALK

So far we have discovered that talk varies according to who you are
and to whom you are talking and in which social environment you
find yourself and the communication itself is very much affected by
your tone, manner, rhythm and style of delivery. Now before we
get onto the central issues, which are The Dichotomy of Dialogue
and The Twins of Talk, we can quickly dispose of the subject matter
of conversation. This need not take long because we only talk about
very few things, as listed below:

Willy:	sex
Welly:	sport
Woolly:	intellectual matters
Wiley:	people
Wallet:	money
Wally:	tomfoolery

'To hear people talk,' wrote W. H. Auden. 'You would think
that in their free time, i.e. when not engaged in action or directed
thinking, they were concerned with nothing but sex, prestige and
money.' This is not always the case, as in Nancy Mitford's *Love in
a Cold Climate* when one young socialite says to another: 'Do
you think about dresses and hats all the time – even in church?
I do.'

2 THE MENTAL MARRIAGE OF PLAY AND PURPOSE

I will now tell you the secret of life, the key to happiness. It is the marriage between Mr Purpose and Miss Play, which needs to happen in your mind.

A lot of people bring off this happy balance in the honeymoon period of their youth, but later a separation, if not divorce, can take place as one or other of the two parties gain ascendancy. More often than not, play is sacrificed on the altar of purpose as routine, duty and ambition take their toll.

> All work and no play
> Make Jack a dull boy.
> All play and no work
> Make him a bit of a jerk.

Obviously the ultimate questions that life throws at us are 'why?' and 'what is the point?' Depression lasts for as long as you think that there is no point. Have you ever heard people talk and mistaken it merely for sound? I call it white noise.

Do you ever look around you and think you are better off with silence? What is the point of all this verbal effort if you take away the pleasure principle, which in itself has no meaning? Death is all play and no pleasure, but it is also all purpose and no play. Look at those mirthless religious fanatics killing people for their own good. Pity those workaholics chasing the pot of gold at the end of their lives.

A person without culture is at the mercy of purpose. This was Rex Mottram's problem in *Brisdeshead Revisited*. He was a successful entrepreneur at the prime of his life and he managed to win the heart of Julia Flyte, an aristocratic beauty tired of too much play. She was attracted to Rex for his crude energy and his knowledge of the mechanisms of the world, but after a year of marriage she eventually discovered that 'he was something absolutely modern and up-to-date that only this ghastly age could produce. A tiny bit of a man pretending he was whole.' Rex built his whole conscious being on the shifting sands of money, power, popularity and position. Culture is about absolutes – truth, beauty, goodness. Rex was a relativist. Everything he did, said and thought related to whatever thing or person he wanted in the world. His purpose was hollow and not conducive to self-growth.

We are all organic beings. As we get older, we either improve or get worse. Nobody stays the same and the direction you move depends on the habits of mind you either fall into, or impose on yourself. It is a sad fact of life that a lot of people deteriorate. How often have you come across stodgy old fools dead from the neck up, who in their youth at school and at university were quite the thing? *Yet another friend has gone to the wall,* you say sadly to yourself. If that's bad, it's a lot worse when you see the look of disappointment in the face of some old mucker who has outstripped you in later life.

3   WORK LIKE YOU PLAY

The classic trade off in corporate life is more like highway robbery: their money for your soul. What can so easily shrivel up in the long, arduous crawl up the back passage of success is your spirit. The poor little caged creature can topple off its perch or else grow slack and fat, its beak too long in the seed tray. The eagle has become a parrot. The middle classes go into management, but be warned by what Kipling says is the price of such promotion: 'Wi' these to oversee, ye'll note I've little time to burn on social repartee.'

Look at the casualty rate amongst even the best, the ones who will have shown great quality to achieve success. Stagecoach millionaire Ann Gloag ruefully described the price of her millions: 'You might find this hard to believe but when I was a girl, I was always laughing.'

'What are you doing?' said a relation of mine (who has been highly successful in his chosen career) to his playful teenage children.

'Having fun,' said one of his teenage children. 'Do you remember that? FUN!'

There is a New Age community in the Highlands of Scotland called the Findhorn Community, which is devoted to resuscitating the spirit. It attracts people who have lost their way in life. They get up to all sorts of alternative practices, howling at the moon and balancing crystals on their foreheads for all I know. They certainly talk to plants, which apparently respond by growing doubly large. Another example of the power of words, I tentatively suggest.

I am told there are a fair number of self-made millionaires amongst their group. It seems strange that after you sacrifice yourself to make your millions you have to take classes in how to be yourself again. In finding your fortune you have lost yourself, so you have to spend your fortune to find yourself again.

The money to which you devoted your early manhood is absolutely irrelevant in a genuine community like Findhorn because the only thing that is valued there is how well you get on with your neighbour. Findhorn is a village without a mansion. It does not even have superior housing.

I asked my Russian neighbour, Shenka, what it was like attending a banquet given by her successful brother in Moscow for his business friends, acquaintances, colleagues and, of course, enemies who needed to be kept close. She said: 'boring and frightening'. She explained that relations between people operated according to the principle of a Power Pyramid. The men were only interested in maintaining their cool and recommending themselves to people further up the pecking order. The women were mere appendages. They were expensively dressed trollops, she said with soviet disdain. Everyone was nouveau riche. Not a drop of culture evident anywhere.

Finally Shenka managed to engage a man in conversation, only for him to abandon the dialogue within half a dozen remarks. He simply stopped. He just could not summon the energy or the interest to respond. She had nothing to offer him and he was not interested in what Shenka was saying, which was nothing about money. Later her brother upbraided her for not being normal.

What is so destructive about success is that it so rarely happens overnight. In the long years spent in pursuit of it, you can fall into habits that are good for business but bad for the soul. The most insidious, or is it invidious, habit of all is to be permanently extracting things from other people: mostly information, but sometimes money, and this leads to a terribly exploitative attitude.

Time is money, so you cannot waste it on gossip with friends or you will go out of business. Workaholics must learn to become lazy again. The Babongo tribesmen of the Gabon work and hunter-gather just four hours a day. Otherwise they hang out together smoking and chatting and playing with their children. 'Unlike us,' says documentary presenter Bruce Perry.

Humans are heroes but the circumstances of their lives, especially in the modern world with its unique demands, can put them to sleep. The mechanical business of life, especially their jobs, can turn them into zombies. Television merely extends the coma. Lots of books and films act as a wake-up call. Think of even a silly film like *Pretty Woman*. It took contact with a prostitute to make self-made millionaire Richard Gere wake up to the fact that he had degenerated into a money-making robot.

4 DON'T GO THROUGH THE MOTIONS

D. H. Lawrence devoted his whole oeuvre to this theme: What is life and what is merely existence and how does one get from one to the other? In *Women in Love* all five main characters start off dissatisfied with lives that look perfectly acceptable from the outside.

Listen to these quotes, all expressing the same frustrations in different ways. One of the protagonists, Gerald, comes from a family of industrialists. 'We can do things – but we can't get on with life at all. It's curious – a family failing,' Gerald says, and the narrator elaborates that 'he who triumphed in the world, he became more and more hollow in his vitality.' The other male protagonist, Birkin, is a teacher, but he has similar frustrations: 'I am becoming quite dead-alive, nothing but a word-bag,' says Birkin of himself.

Words are necessary to strike out of this psychic inertia. But words spoken in order to conform with society's conventions or, worse still, words that are put into your mouth to sell product, are a waste of breath. They merely serve to exacerbate this feeling of being part of the living dead. 'Either you think – or else others have to think for you and take power from you, prevent and discipline your natural tastes, civilise and sterilise you,' comments Scott Fitzgerald in *Tender is the Night.* Find your own language. Think your own thoughts. Use your own words. Otherwise life is just meaningless.

In *Women in Love* two of Lawrence's characters, Birkin and Ursula, succeed in re-animating themselves, breaking out of mechanical existence and finding a real life. They do this by achieving real connection through love, friendship and knowledge.

The other three characters are sidetracked. Ultimate cowardice and personal vanity provide insurmountable obstacles. They do not have the guts to risk genuine encounter. They merely flirt with the possibility. Hermione especially would not fully open herself up to experience, necessary to achieve personal growth: 'All the while this passive, tortured woman piled up her own defences of aesthetic knowledge, and culture, and world-visions and disinteredness. All her life she has sought to make herself invulnerable.'

That is why most people stay slaves to the system. They do not want the feelings of discomfort and general upheaval that disturb a person during a period of transition. Then there are the people at the other end of the spectrum, who have no purpose in life other than the pursuit of pleasure through play. Because of our social conditioning which stems from the Anglo-Saxon protestant work ethic, there is a tendency for the rest of the population to look down upon what is called the idle rich – but, as Mary North, a character in *Tender is the Night,* says: 'All people want is to have a good time.'

Of course, that is not as easy as it sounds, even if you have got enough money to buy any amount of time you want. The hero of *Tender Is The Night,* Dick Diver himself, despite being one of those magnetic people the Gods have blessed with all the social graces, eventually cannot handle permanent leisure and regrets having been emotionally blackmailed into giving up his day job.

Indeed the message of the book is that every man needs a purpose and once it has gone, he is finished. Dick Diver gave up writing his treatise on some aspect of psychology in order to take care of his rich and beautiful, but deeply neurotic, young wife. Having eventually cured her by his constant care and support, she leaves him for another man. The sure sign of the success of his ministrations is that she finally feels self confident enough to leave him. The price of wealth and the cost of leisure was his energy and his sense of purpose. He ends the book adrift and abandoned by all who had followed him.

5   ARE YOU A SOCIALITE OR A THEORIST?

As you probably know by now, I admire people who are socially adept and I am certainly amazed at what it takes to be a 100 per cent socialite. I am not really a party man and I like to restrict holidays to a long weekend. Enforced idleness makes me jumpy. But then I freely admit I am an undeveloped human being, which is what has made me write this book in the first place. It is time I addressed the real issues in my life instead of permanently postponing them. Perhaps if I had taken action earlier to correct myself, I would still have a wife.

As I have said before, it is much easier to do than to be. Workers do, socialites are. So as a worker, I genuinely look up to a socialite. In fact, not only does socialising demand more of you as a fully rounded human being than working, but according to Professor Robert Winston in his book, *The Human Mind,* there is no activity more mentally demanding than socialising. Scans reveal that conversation activates almost the whole of your brain. He describes socialising as 'one of the most taxing parts of human existence'.

Certainly my own personal experience of socialites is that in certain obvious respects they tend to be brighter than the rest of us. They have a hundred times the practice in the difficult art of conversation. Practice, as they say, makes perfect. The brain responds to stimulation and nobody is more stimulated than a socialite. While the rest of us are slumped in front of the television after an exhausting day repeating ourselves in the work place, your classic socialite is reaching peak performance. Their days are mostly spent in preparation for society at night.

The bird brain of the social butterfly is a myth. Yes, I would not ask a socialite to investigate any problem in detail. Their brilliance lies in their ability to skate lightly and brightly across the surface of things. 'There was always an unspoken pressure to keep to the surface of things,' writes Liza Campbell in her book *Title Deeds* about the experience of having been brought up by her father, the Earl of Cawdor. That is a type of intelligence, a facility that makes for entertainment. Like comedians, they are brilliant at summing up a situation.

Of course not all socialites are members of the idle rich. You can be a coveted dinner party guest without being absurdly wealthy, but serious party people do tend to avoid nine-five jobs. As such it takes a huge amount of self-discipline to live the life of the idle rich and avoid sinking into a life of dissipation. They can easily end up as one of those sad and seedy swingers who still go to nightclubs way past their bedtime.

'A time comes when they are no longer attractive or in good form. They can't drink any more, and they still hanker after women, only they have to pay and make compromises in order to escape from their loneliness: they have become figures of fun. They grow sentimental and hard to please. I have seen many who have gone the same way,' writes Françoise Sagan in *Bonjour Tristesse*.

The ancient Greeks got it right 2,000 years ago. We should all aim for The Golden Mean. One version of it much favoured by our adrenaline and coke-fuelled, pre-credit crunch, city traders used to be: 'Work hard! Play hard!' That sounds too exhausting for me. My personal mantra is not to work harder than you play.

7 ARE YOU AN IDEAS PERSON OR A PEOPLE PERSON?

Some people theorise about society, other people enjoy it. The social theorisers of the world are those who want to change society for the better. A socialite, on the other hand, just wants to succeed in society. Theorists want to alter the rules of the game, socialites just wants to win the game.

All hippies, crusaders and revolutionaries (whether they were fascists or Christians or communists), are interested in the theory of society. Most people, however, are socialites. They don't concern themselves with the rights and wrongs, the fairness and unfairness of society. What they are interested in is how best to prosper within the system, as it currently operates in its economic, political, social and cultural form. Writers like D. H. Lawrence, whose entire body of work was devoted to the question of how best to live your life, was par excellence a theorist.

The danger about being fascinated by the theory is that you can find yourself thinking about life instead of living it. The risk about being a socialite is boredom because, as Socrates says: 'The unexamined life is not worth living.' It is ultimately meaningless and I think you can come a cropper in old age. You will not be surprised to hear that what I think you should do is strike a balance between thinking and socialising.

What I have grandly called the Duality of Talk is the big question you have got to ask yourself. Are you by nature and nurture a theoriser or a socialite? Are you the sort of person who is always thinking of ways that the system in which you find yourself can be improved, or do you look about you to finds ways to enjoy yourself? How ambitious are you? Are you dreaming of millions? Are you driven by some beautiful ideal or do you want to wangle an extra ten minutes on your coffee break? Are you planning a practical joke to play on your unsuspecting boss, or do you dream of impressing him so much he has to promote you? Do you want to do good for the world or just be good to yourself and your friends?

The other day, I asked a friend of mine, Debs, whether she had anything exciting currently going on in her life. She said nothing leapt to mind but she was looking forward to a fancy dress party in ten days time wherever everybody had to dress up as a famous musician. She was planning to go either as Dolly Parton or June Carter, Johnny Cash's eventual wife. How different she was to me, I thought. I always have some private pet project on the go that gives me a permanent low level sense of excitement. My current buzz is my pub in Brixton, which I plan to make the best medium sized music venue in London.

My hairdresser friend is a socialite. I am a theoriser. My natural style of conversation is analytic. Debs' is narrative or incidental. She takes delight in foible. I am crucified by the question *why?* I always look for patterns and explanations and consequently am drawn to behaviour that defies reason. I am fascinated, for example, by the phenomenon of people who lie even if they know they are bound to be found out. I am amazed by vindictive people. I am impressed by people who lose their temper in public. I am riveted by hypocrisy. I am astonished by people who concentrate on the miniature when big things all about them are ready for the taking. I am charmed by people whose every move is not calculated. There is a foolishness that is enchanting.

8   WHY DO WE SECRETLY LOVE OUR ENEMIES?

I think theorisers who can get over their adolescent contempt for socialites end up admiring them. They grow to love there. You can see from Evelyn Waugh's early books how mercilessly he satirised aristocratic society, but he ended up buying a mansion himself, dressing up almost as a caricature of a country gent and adopting the life and manner he had previously pilloried.

So often people perform total crossovers in late middle age. How many trade union leaders and left-wing radicals have ended up in the House of Lords? They are accused of hypocrisy, of betraying their principles and selling out to the enemy. Not a bit of it, or maybe just a bit of it, but a lot of it is explained by a learning to appreciate alternative, even contradictory, attitudes.

Don't we all secretly love what we do not have? Initially, of course, we are afraid of it, then as we grow in confidence we fall in love with it. I freely admit that beneath a thin veneer of superiority, I was born and brought up in fear of the working class. And I have, without a doubt, grown to admire it.

I think every white collar individual is unsettled by the juggernaut of blue collar energy. Power comes from connection. No wonder workers have a power denied to people who merely use words for a living. Making and creating tangible objects gives the working class a vitality that those from the other side of the social divide can only pretend. Compare the tame self-conscious chants of the middle class crowd at Wimbledon to the roar of the crowd at Wembley.

What used to be called 'class warfare' was really a love affair. Commentators put it down to envy and they were right, but you don't envy something you don't want, and desire is a form of love. I do envy the working classes and in some way I believe they envy us. Certainly East End boy desires West End girl.

Also there is a fear and respect for educated use of language. You only have to see the cowed behaviour of criminals in court. Irrespective of their background, they cower when confronted with the magisterial language of the law. It's certainly not the odd copper that frightens them. Brixton has taught me that.

Opposites attract. I remember the actor Nigel Havers saying that his father, a key figure in the legal profession, was delighted he had gone into acting, which compared to law might be considered rather a lightweight activity. Copying other people and memorising dialogue – which even children can do very well, as is proven in lots of films – is unlikely to impress a high court judge. Yet Havers senior thought Nigel's choice of career was a hoot: so unlike his own studious, sensible profession.

The best, most dangerous, and certainly most entertaining marriage (and also the least likely to succeed) is one between opposites who have surrendered to their mutual attraction. My marriage was like that. Sarah had everything I didn't, including startling good looks, a first class academic brain, a playful mind and the best legs on campus. I met her at one university and lost her in another, twenty years later while she was upgrading her degree to a PHD. At the time I called it Perplexed, Humiliated and Dumped but now I can see that I was partly to blame.

I remember distinctly, on about the fourth day of our honeymoon, realising that at the superficial level of social banter our conversational styles were incompatible. Her humour was surreal, verbal and marvellously pointless. Mine was slapstick, driven by narrative and observation. She had such a light dexterous touch and she was full of fancy. Most of all, she was freewheeling. She liked to accompany somebody on a comic conceit, capping and complimenting what the other person brought to the party of entertainment. I, on the other hand, can make people laugh, but I need total control. Other people's amusing interjections I can do without. We shared plenty of purpose in our marriage. The play was the problem and Sarah felt she had to suppress that part of herself to protect my ego. I wrote a rhyming poem about how a bad marriage goes wrong.

The six stages of Marriage
Enthuse
Amuse
Use
Abuse
Refuse
Lose

Mine was a good marriage and the real reason it eventually failed is the child inside me bullied the child inside her. She always had to be amused by me. This book is my attempt to remedy myself so I do not repeat my mistake with my next wife, who does not know it yet but is being currently lined up for a takeover bid, sorry: merger. The whole point of getting married is to know who to marry next time you get married. Also, how to behave second time round. Quite frankly, how can you know all this in youth when you're ignorant, or early middle age when you're distracted? I'm fifty-four and only now am I finally ready to get married.

One of the noisiest if not downright pugilistic of marriages in the history of literature was between D. H. Lawrence and his wife Frieda, whose personalities were polar opposite. She was fat, sexually carnivorous and idle. He was a skinny, puritanical workaholic. And yet their marriage worked because, as Frieda said: 'With Lawrence I found what I wanted – all the exuberance of my childhood came back to me.' No greater gift can a man bestow upon his wife.

9   PETER PAN MUST NEVER GROW UP

Finding your inner child might well be a self-help book cliché but clichés tend to be true, or else we would not repeat them. The child we are looking for in this context is the cheeky little monkey without a sensible bone in its body. Everyone is a funny one. Bogged down by an adult lifetime of duty, cunning, calculation and convention, we seek to resuscitate what is random in us: the trickster, the joker, and the artful dodger.

My all-time favourite children's film is *Hook*, not just because it manages to provide the viewer with the key to relocating the child within himself, but also because the hero, Peter Pan, manages as an adult to have a wife and five fantasy girlfriends – a fairy, three mermaids and a childhood sweetheart – all of whom he kisses at one point or another in the film, yet never misses a heartbeat in his affection for his wife.

This is the ultimate middle class mid-life crisis movie. It gives the complete picture. It argues that despite his infidelities, during this upsetting period of transition, a man's heart is always in his home. What really matters, what is really important, what is his primary psychic task in middle age, is to seek and find his inner child.

In this film Peter Pan has grown up and become a lawyer. His life is ruled by his mobile phone, which continuously goes off. Eventually his long-suffering wife hurls the phone out of the window and Peter ends up being transported back to Neverland, where he proves a grave disappointment to his erstwhile followers, the Lost Boys, who can see he has abandoned all his original zest for life. Even Hook won't deign to fight him, since the battle would be one sided. But the most disappointing thing of all is that Peter has been so tamed by society that he has forgotten how to trade insults with any degree of skill or venom.

Now this is the crucial point in the film, and psychologically it is very accurate: the big breakthrough comes when he is exposed to a classic playground scene where the bad boys are slagging one another off. Something stirs in Peter's mind, some child's natural impulse to give as good as it gets. Abuse is the key. Polite society can get you money, position and comfort, but if you want to feel like a child again, you have got to start getting rude.

And I'll tell you why. Because it's real. The fact is we don't naturally like strangers. It is manners that cause us shake hands and say *how do you do*. Until we have got over our automatic and immediate disquiet, what we naturally want to do is ignore, avoid or possibly punch the person. We are frightened of the unknown and somebody we have never met before is by definition an unknown quantity. We are not much better behaved towards people we do know, all of whom are ridiculous – I've never met one person who wasn't – and so our natural response, untampered by social convention, is ridicule.

Working class people operating outside the bounds of polite society are thoroughly rude to one another. They take the permanent piss. The child is present and incorrect down the pit, on the terraces and in the pub. The man on hourly rate does not talk for a living. He does not need to be polite.

I am not advocating bad manners. Far from it, I abhor bad manners in conversation. There are three cardinal rules that should never be flouted. Never interrupt. Never monopolise. Never contradict.

However, the point I am making is that manners are not natural and if you are trying to regain the spontaneity you naturally had as a child, before the onset of puberty brought about the curse of self consciousness, then you need to know how to dispense with certain manners. As with everything, the Golden Rule is balance. You need to know how to be well mannered and also bloody rude, on purpose and in play.

It takes guts and imagination to break through decades of social conditioning to reactivate the fearless playground imp in us all. To my eternal shame I found myself embodying the acme of mannerly consideration on the occasion when I eventually re-met the person who had absconded with my wife. I was queuing for a taxi at Inverness airport and my wife had just dropped him off to let him catch the next plane to London. He used to be a friend of mine before I discovered he was a better friend of my wife's. Unbelievably, I actually found myself waving hello to him. He then offered my wife as a possible lift back home to save me the price of a taxi. He told me that if I was quick maybe I could catch her before she left the airport car park. I think I might even have thanked him for being so kind as to have offered my wife back to me, if only as a temporary means of transport and aid to economy. Manners maketh man a blithering grinning idiot half the time.

10 THINGS MATTER

One way back to his linguistic origins for the educated man is relearning how to take delight in the particular. This can come through developing a genuine love of a subject, when you want to know every little thing about it, not just the rules of nature that govern its being. See how a child can love an object like a marble, a doll or a stamp, irrespective of its value. That sensibility is what the grown man needs to recapture because appearance matters as much as reality. It is the other half of life, taking up as much of your time and occupying as much of your mind.

Sylvia Plath noted to herself in her journals: 'The abstract kills, the concrete saves.' She means a poem dies on its feet if it is made up only of abstractions. God is in the detail. A poem needs actuality. It must have flesh and blood and arms and legs to come alive as work of art. John O'Donohue correctly describes creativity as the tension that exists between clay and the spirit.

A writer cannot merely inhabit some intellectual bubble, floating free of its connection with the million irregularities of actual living. Ted Hughes, who was president of a writers' community called Arvon, a branch of which my sister and I set up in Scotland, told me that the ivory tower is the kiss of death to a writer. He said that many a writer never fulfilled the promise of their first novel because they suddenly start thinking of themselves self-consciously as 'writers'. A more useful way of thinking yourself was as a spy. You must not cut yourself off from your material, which is to be found in the rough and tumble of ordinary life and which you don't find in the exclusive world of your study, he advised. Of course, being a nature poet he was lucky in not needing a day job to access his material. He just had to toddle out into the countryside.

Desert Arabs recognise the importance of physical objects. They put on a sub-turban, which is a tie around their heads to keep the turban from slipping and falling off, and they liken this fixture to the practice of what they call hobbling a camel. There are no trees in the desert and so to prevent the camels from wandering off in the middle of the night the Desert Arabs tie their camels' back legs together. This serves as a reminder for them to keep their minds on the here and now and not to let it wander off into fantasy and metaphysics – quite a temptation in the sand and sky eternity of the desert.

In the Muslim tradition you lower your head on your prayer mat so that the heart is above the level of the head for the same reason. The head makes contact with the earth. You need to have your feet on the ground before you put your head in the clouds. I am referring to manual and mental activity.

In mental work your mind is for hire. The company buys your brain for the working day. The problem is that if you are not properly grounded, linguistic habits formed at work can spill over into your private life so that a lawyer can talk like a lawyer even when he is at the seaside with a bucket and spade. There was an article in *The Sunday Times* about hardworking and very successful business executives being interviewed about taking early retirement and living off their hard-earned capital and income.

'We have done this for twenty years,' said Carol Caley, the top fund manager of Mercury Asset Management. 'It's been enormous fun and a great privilege, but there is another side to the balance sheet.' I think by 'balance sheet', she means life.

Another successful business executive, Patricia Hodge, said later in the same article: 'Some people may want to pack it all in and sail around the world, but a high proportion of businessmen still have lot of juice left, as well as intellectual and physical capital.' By 'intellectual capital', she means ideas.

They can escape the company, but not the mindset and the language that goes with it and so they are bound for life. You get into habits of thinking and talking, from which you cannot take early retirement. It takes conscious time and effort to liberate yourself from these language parameters. Everything you say has a point and, to a certain extent, it is set against the clock. Idle chat, as in one person talking to another for no apparent reason, is discouraged because (as is drummed into you from the first moment you step into your office), time is money.

In manual work the opposite is true. You can't physically work the sixty minutes of an hour. You probably can't physically work more than four hours in eight. So there is a lot of time each day spent recouping your strength to do the next thing. Talk alleviates the dullness of this downtime, which is why manual workers are such social experts.

11 PROFESSIONAL LANGUAGE

On the other hand, there is a lot to recommend the professional life. The gift of becoming a lawyer, for example, is that you require the language of control. It is the best verbal training in the world. As an arts student you can come out of university with a nice mix of narrative and analytic linguistic skills, then you immerse yourself in your legal studies. It's as dry as parchment and who cares about the million laws or those myriad sub clauses? The way actually to enjoy your legal studies is to see them for what they are – a massive linguistic exercise. Every profession has its language and there eventually resides the pleasure of it. If you are an accountant, for example, you should say: 'Ah yes, I speak four languages: English, French, accountancy and a smattering of law.' People dismiss a profession's language as jargon, but in reality it is the most appropriate, effective, accurate way of dealing with the issues that crop up in that particular field.

Look at how inefficient a professional language is before it is fully formed. The language of literary criticism, for example, was in its infancy when Samuel Johnson was writing his *Lives of the Poets*. It was considered a seminal work at the time but compared to contemporary critical works it is a rambling, shambolic, amateur piece of unproven, self-opinionated polemic. It would barely get a lower second if it was handed in today as a dissertation for an English degree. The language had not yet been worked out so, though original, Samuel Johnson was handicapped and it shows in how heavy handed was his expression.

Obviously there is more to a profession than its language. There is also a key to each one. The key to advertising, for example, is puns; the key to accountancy and law is lists; to song writing, vowels; to business, ratios; to science, comparisons; to academia, footnotes; to religion, imagination; to sport, repetition; and to journalism, reduction.

Sebastian Faulks, the brilliant author of *Birdsong*, used to be a journalist. In his book *Engleby* he writes that journalism can be boiled down to this: 'You ask a question and write down the answer. You repeat the process a few times. Then you see what all the answers add up to, put them in sequential order with a simple linking narrative and go to the pub.' He is right about the pub. I forgot to mention it.

The danger of the professions is that you can find yourself limited to people of your own linguistic orientation, not just socially, but in every other way as well: lawyers marry lawyers and beget little lawyers who in turn have even smaller grandlawyers. In her Pulitzer Prize winning novel *Foreign Affairs*, Alison Lurie describes how a bunch of actors at a smart London cocktail party 'like most actors, were uninterested in meeting anyone not in their own profession.'

That's the beauty of living in the country. You are at the mercy of your neighbours, who can come from completely different linguistic backgrounds. It makes you multilingual, more capable of associating with people of different types.

12 BIG AND SMALL TALK

Some people have a real problem with small talk; others can't cope with big talk. The British in general, and the Scots in particular, have a horror of pretension. In Europe there is a class called the intelligentsia. We, in this country, call them the 'chattering classes' because it down plays their importance. No Englishman in his right mind would ever have the audacity to call himself an intellectual. It would be social suicide. I doubt the Brit exists who has used the word 'existentialism' in mixed company, by which I mean a group of people from mixed linguistic backgrounds.

People have got egos to protect. If all else fails, simply removing yourself from a room where you are being made to feel a fool is crude but effective. We have a very powerful language that can easily overcome you – rob you in a very brief space of time of all the self-confidence you have so painstakingly built up over the course of your life to date.

The English language, for example, has twice the number of words as the French language. It is no wonder we used to beat them in battle two or three times a century and even when we were friends, as in the last century, we had to bail them out twice against superior forces. You might think that power comes out of the barrel of a gun, but its use of language that persuade people to pick up arms in the first place. Words make armies. Hitler knew that.

I am one of those people who relax with 'big talk'. That does not mean to say I am cleverer than my bar staff who, by and large, prefer a joke or a quip or some nice light abuse. It is just that big talk about the existence of God or the analysis of human behaviour or some political debate does not really matter. It's safe. It's impersonal. You can't do any harm with abstract opinions about war, philosophy, or religion. You don't have to apologise for God not existing. None of it is your fault. The words used in debate are great big impersonal ones like 'justification', 'imply', 'tendency', or 'requirement'.

Watch a late night arts review programme on television for vocab inspiration. Obviously meaning helps in big talk, but it's not essential. Ambiguity abounds in the arts. It's positively *de rigueur* in modern poetry.

But the point I am really trying to make is that there is a freedom in intellectual exchange. It allows you to take time to develop a point. In repartee all you have is a heartbeat to find just the right dozen words to cap or respond in kind to the verbal volley fired at you by some competing wag.

Don't think I come to this subject as a novice. A hundred essays at sixth form and then university have equipped me and the rest of my kind with the perfect training to feel comfortable during 'big talk'. What is the first question that occurs to a student when confronted with the prospect of having to write an essay? *How fascinating? What a target rich area for research? What a golden opportunity to develop my thinking on this matter?* No, the question is always: *how many words can I get away with?*

One of the greatest skills we pick up at university is the ability to waffle. How else are you going to earn huge salaries as a professional in later life if you cannot spin a subject for ten times the time it should really take? There is not a business plan in the world whose essential points you cannot fit on one side of an A4 piece of paper, but it would not raise a penny of investors' money or bankers' loan because everybody expects a business plan to be at least as thick as a magazine. So that is one page of relevance and ninety-nine pages of waffle.

The ultimate prize for waffle goes to lawyers, who in many ways you just have to admire. But then, they do have an incentive. They are paid oodles by the hour. In fact I doubt there is a lawyer in the UK who is paid less than a pound a minute and some get a pound a second. How else do you explain the open and shut case of O. J. Simpson lasting more than an afternoon, considering his DNA was all over the offending glove? Yet they not only stretched the case over months, they got him off. It is not often you get two bites of the cake, but lawyers are magicians and the spells they cast are woven with words.

What puts the frighteners on me is small talk. Try as I might, I cannot really get a purchase on it. When some apparently perfectly sane person starts telling me about a foreign holiday or the age of their dog or some incident involving a traffic warden, I can't help thinking: 'What is the point of what you are saying?'

The secret to small talk is genuinely caring about other people. So when a friend says that they are going to Cyprus in a few weeks time on holiday, ideally it should give you a feeling of pleasure on their behalf. It's called empathy. That piece of information about their proposed holiday trip tells you nothing you did not know before about human behaviour. It has absolutely no cultural, political or social significance, but it should mean something to you because you care about the people involved.

Always suspect a man with no small talk of not really caring about his fellow man as an individual. Oh yes I'm big on social theory, but do I really care about the people I call my friends? The smaller the talk, the bigger the heart. 'I had to learn how to enjoy and to 'do' intimate relationships. My tip, which I had to learn myself, is to talk about apparent trivia,' says Edward Straw, the chairman of Relate, the charity devoted to saving marriages.

Small talk is as important as big talk. You want to be able to see the wood AND the trees. Without the trees there would be no wood. To really know about a wood, you first need to know about a tree. You can see a wood, but you can't climb it. That's what a tree has over a wood. There is a level of experience that exists in the local, in the individual, in the miniature that is not to be found in the whole. And there is a humility needed to access it.

You should be grateful for the little things in life, recommends Fr Slavko Barbaric, a spiritual adviser at Medjugorje, the town in Croatia where Our Lady is said to have appeared to six young visionaries on a daily basis at twenty to seven over the last twenty years. Fr Slavko tells us of the importance of appreciating 'the smallest of things'. 'Think of the story of Adam and Eve – they received everything from the Lord, but in one moment, they forgot, they became blind to what the Lord had given them: they wanted to sin, they felt they had to sin in the hope of receiving even more. They became blind. This is the deepest form of atheism. Who can give everything to a selfish person? When will a selfish person ever say thank you? If he were to be given the whole world, it would not be enough. When can a proud person say thank you? Even if you do everything for him, it will not be enough. He who is humble sees the others, he sees the smallest of things, he starts thanking,' says Fr Slavko.

13 DIRECT AND INDIRECT TALK

A lot of manners are primarily designed to avoid embarrassment. We are in fact the only animals on the planet who suffer from that excruciating feeling. Have you ever seen a dog blush? Dogs do not have to chat up bitches successfully to have sex with them. They never get stumped for a reply. 'Woof' probably covers all eventualities. A dog is blissfully unaware of the million social niceties and nuances that plague our consciousness.

Being polite is easier than being direct or genuine. Of course, a direct encounter between two people is riveting because both people have to be fully awake and alive to what is happening between them. This kind of intercourse naturally happens in moments of high emotion – otherwise, especially in high society, we take great pains to avoid it. The vast majority of social conversation is second-hand. It will be comment of one sort or another or it will come in the form of narrative. It is safe to tell a story to somebody because it is not happening as you speak.

It is safe for the narrator because he knows in advance what he is going to say to the listener, who has the luxury of not having to respond for a while, and is quite comfortable with this recognisable format.

Read this scene from *Brideshead Revisited* that perfectly illustrates the limitations of indirect talk. Charles Ryder is trying to comfort Julia Flyte after her brother has just told her that she and Charles cannot possibly stay under the same roof as his fiancée because they are living in sin. Julia has rushed out of the house in tears and Charles has joined her at the ornamental fountain.

'It's like the setting of a comedy,' I said. 'Scene: a Baroque fountain in a nobleman's grounds. Act one, sunset; act two, dusk; act three, moonlight. The characters keep assembling at the fountain for no very clear reason.'

'Comedy?'

'Drama. Tragedy. Farce. What you will. This is the reconciliation scene.'

'Was there a quarrel?'

'Estrangement and misunderstanding in act two.'

'Oh, don't talk in that damned bounderish way. Why must you see everything second-hand? Why must this be a play?'

I have a friend, Richard Harrington, who gave up the professional life to become a sheep farmer in Ross-shire in the Highlands of Scotland and I wondered about the cultural gap. How would he, an Oxford graduate and top London lawyer, cope with the rough and tumble of the agricultural world? He replied enigmatically that he preferred the company and conversation of people who lived, no matter how basic the subject matter – and you don't get more basic than sheep – to people who talked cleverly about people who lived. Theory was not his bag. I quite correctly took that as a personal put-down. His answer made me think of how, in Jane Austen's *Pride and Prejudice,* one woman says to another: 'We don't live and therefore we have to philosophise.'

Children are direct because they don't know what anything much means. They react instantly with emotion and they take delight in the actuality of things. The problem about education is that it can make us more interested in the means than the end. On the other hand education gives us some pleasurable and entertaining tools, like vocabulary.

The eye-opener that university provided for me was entry to the world of analysis, the prime product of indirect talk. It transformed my life. Instead of saying that I thoroughly disliked a person because he had behaved badly, I could all of a sudden discuss his unpleasantness in terms of neurosis. Not only could I appear to feel sorry for my enemy, I could also lay claim to the apparent objectivity of the concerned observer: my real antipathy blissfully camouflaged.

That is the beauty of words and logic. As long as I used the Latin-based language of psychology and I conducted my observations in the spirit of enquiry, I could assassinate the fellow's character with perfect equanimity. Psychobabble is the way we of the chattering classes put the knife into one another.

The other enjoyable form of indirect conversation is discussion of any sort: social, political, cultural comment; and that, as pointed out in the section on big talk, is easy, safe and endless as long as you have mastered the vocabulary. In the index at the back of this book I've provided vocabulary lists for literature, politics and film – the three most popular dinner party topics. Five hundred words just about cover each topic.

14 PAST AND PRESENT TALK

'Few people are actually able to inhabit their present time because they are too stressed and rushed,' writes John O'Donohue in *Anam Cara*. People spend much of their time talking in the past tense because it does not involve using your imagination, which, if you are not accustomed to it, is an exercise of will and daring. It is the difference between reportage and repartee. In terms of television it is the difference between a repeat program and a live show.

It is obviously far easier to tell somebody about something that has happened than to make it all up, or, even more difficult, to respond in kind and on time to somebody else's inventions. The highest form of conversation is two people accompanying one another on some improvised fanciful conceit. You can see it first-hand any night of the week on the Jonathan Ross show, or anything with Graham Norton, Stephen Fry or Paul Merton in it.

There you will see consummate performers inhabiting the present for the brilliant stuff, and dipping into the past to knock off an occasional humorous anecdote.

How many times a week do I sit staring at the television with a silly smile on my face, being charmed by marvellous people I don't know and will never meet? With my friends it is a lot more guarded because I feel I must at all times protect my fragile ego. I must never be wrong footed in conversation.

The other people to whom I listen with envy and admiration are my teenage children when they are having the *craic* with their friends. They have the brilliance of youth, before routine has taken the edge off their wit. To hear them with their peer group is to witness masters of play. They have never in their lives done any sustained, single-minded, repetitive work. Instead their attitude to study is to get it out of the way as quickly as possible so that they can concentrate on their social lives. They are on the look-out at all times for the opportunity to play or trick or tease and they devote oceans of leisure time to talking with their friends either one to one, in a small group or in a party. They even have spare time to contemplate the universal questions. They can sit for hours, with or without alcohol, chewing the comic cud with one another. The point of this book is to show you the way back to the verbal exuberance of irresponsible youth, tempered with the wisdom and consideration of age.

People can be interesting and boring at the same time because they fail to bring their subject, no matter how inherently interesting, into the present. It happened to me the other day in the pub. This fellow told me all about Columbia. My man was just relaying facts to me. I might just as well have been listening to a radio documentary. It demanded nothing from me except a pair of functioning ears. The man himself was merely down loading his memory. It was like a pre-recorded performance. These were the ten fascinating things he said about Columbia, yet he had me looking over his shoulder with envy at the fun my staff were having at the other end of the bar:

1. The Columbian style of political graffiti is dead pan humour.
2. They call their country Lacombia: The Mad Place.
3. His girlfriend's step aunt was the runner-up in Columbia's presidential elections.
4. The USA funds the Columbian army thanks to the cocaine trade.
5. It is twice the size of France. It has got the Amazon running through it. It has mountains and a Caribbean coastline. What beauty! What variety! It's got coffee, oil, beef cattle, and cocaine and yet it is the fourth biggest recipient of US aid after Israel, Saudi Arabia and Egypt.
6. Drug barons have been replaced by politicised terrorist groups – three of them.
7. Oldest democracy in South America. Been going one hundred years.
8. Army limited in size by constitution. If needed to expand for war or anti-terrorist campaign, extra money voted on an *ad hoc* basis so that after the emergency, army can revert to pre-agreed size.
9. Population is Spanish and Indian mix. Nobody with grey hair. Blacks on the Columbian Caribbean cost.
10. Columbian coasts on both oceans: Atlantic and Pacific.

What he failed to do was make all this information relate to me, his listener. Compare that to the effect of what happened next. A woman came up to me and said I looked as if I was in need of relief. Suddenly my mind was racing, searching for a reply. She hadn't said anything particularly interesting, but my mind was activated – I'm wondering whether she means the *double entendre*, and in what tone I ought to respond. I was involved, directly and in the present tense.

Incidentally, all great ladies' men, all the seducers and persuaders of the world, know when suddenly to switch on the present tense having reassured their prey into a false sense of security with some nice easy past participles. But if they suddenly want to excite a woman, they must go to the here and now. You can suddenly say, as the womaniser says in *The Unbearable Lightness of Being*: 'Strip!'

They are called chat up lines, and adolescents fantasise about them. Films are full of them. What was it that Humphrey Bogart said to Ingrid Bergman in *Casablanca*? Whatever it was, he will have closed the deal with a neat bit of present tense. In fact film, which is all about the many different and dramatic ways in which people connect with one another, is mostly conducted in the present tense.

If you want to talk in the permanent past tense, you can interest and entertain people as well but you will fail to make real connection with them. Dreamers, fantasists and idealists talk in the future tense, which is another way of avoiding people. My sister-in-law JJ talks in the future pluperfect but then she is positively mystic!

15 HOME AND AWAY TALK

There are two basic impulses in man – security and adventure. The older you get, especially in this hysterical modern world where you are bombarded from all angles by all manner of alien voices, the greater the lure of home. People become reluctant to stray away from their comfort zone and their social circles get smaller. The danger is that they get increasingly narrow minded.

We know the classes think and talk differently, as do the different professions; now, because of accelerated rate of change, great differences of modes of speech between the ages have emerged. So an old person can look upon a neighbourhood youth almost as a foreigner. This was first identified in the sixties, the onset of the modern age, and they coined the phrased: The Generation Gap.

It's testing enough to bridge the sex gap, but worth it because you do actually get a reward – sex. So in our teens we all set about the linguistic business of learning how to chat up girls because we all know that although men fall in love through their eyes, with women it's the ears.

I've got a friend who is highly popular with both sexes. He explained to me: 'I speak English to the boys and French to the girls.' By French, he meant that he resorts to strategically placed compliments, being highly attentive, letting the other person do most of the talking, maintaining continuous *sangfroid* while feigning a certain *je ne sais quoi* and all those nifty little tricks that make those slimy channel hoppers so successful with the opposite sex. Having finally found their life mate, lots of British men revert to type and thereafter socially stick to their own sex. Everybody prefers their own language.

Social situations are divided into home matches, which crudely speaking are where you meet people on your home patch: place of work, familiar social environment or indeed your actual home. Away matches are where you go elsewhere: the less familiar the surroundings, the greater the mental agility required of you. Great socialites can play as well away as at home. And that is what wins championships. Check Manchester United.

Frances Donaldson in her book *Portrait of a Country Neighbour* wrote of the celebrated author, Evelyn Waugh: 'He was far easier in his own home than away.' She describes: 'Three parts misanthrope, one part gregarious and highly curious, he was inclined to like women better than men because they prattle easily.'

Admittedly, because of the solitary nature of their work, writers in particular can be tempted to shut themselves off from the outside world, or reduce it to their satisfaction. Listen to Anais Nin on her lover, the literary genius Henry Miller: 'He, too, lacks confidence. He is uneasy in certain social situations if they are the least bit chic.' In their work writers inhabit their Second Self and a social life is mostly conducted on the surface, which further disadvantages them. Evelyn Waugh liked people of his choice, on his terms, and for limited periods of time. Inevitably, as the years went by, his social circle dwindled because he insisted on every game being a home game.

It is fear of the unfamiliar that we need to combat, or else we can become locked in a vicious circle of under performance – as national football coach Bobby Robson learnt to his cost when managing our national team. Referring to a particularly gifted player who so badly disappointed him when playing for England, Robson said: 'He played nowhere near his club form, like several others. This is what you find as England coach. That there are players who don't cope with pressure. Who can handle things in their sitting room but can't handle going to meet the Queen at the palace. You've got to find out about these players because they'll let you down. They'll crumble on the day. They'll shirk the responsibility. They'll disappear.'

> 'Wee, sleekit, cow'rin', tim'rous beastie,
> O what a panic's in thy breastie!'

It explains the need, not just the luxury, of drink at parties. It can still the panic in your breast. One good thing about fear though, is that it dispels complacency and inertia. There is such a thing as positive fear. Fear of the Lord, for example, is encouraged in Christianity. It is a perfect preparation for prayer. Reminding yourself of things you're frightened of, like death, can be invigorating.

In times of solitary meditation, you should embrace your fears and make them work for you. They can free your imagination. My personal fear is of the playful wit and effortless small talk paraded most successfully at both ends of the social spectrum: the aristocrats and the manual workers. In their company I feel clodhopping. But I use my fear to imagine typical conversations with very high and low-born people, and it equips me for when I eventually come across them in real life. Practice makes perfect.

Shyness is cowardice. Composure is courage. Everybody is born shy. You only need to look at nature. The first impulse in animals is to run away. It's the same with us. Self-education is the business of overcoming fear by skilful use of the holy trinity of the mind: the intellect, the imagination and the will.

The best way of dealing with fear is by conquest. In a newspaper interview, Michael Caine told Michael Parkinson that as a young boy he was so shy that when any guest came into the house he would hide behind the curtains. Unfortunately the curtains did not fall to the floor, so the only thing they hid was his blushing face, the rest of him remained in full view of everybody else in the room. Michael Caine conquered his shyness by going into public performance. His shyness wilted under the glare of the spotlight.

The second best way of dealing with fear is by circumnavigating it by means of displacement. Lawrence of Arabia, noted for his phenomenal physical bravery, nevertheless could not cope with the drawing room. To escape small talk, he banished himself to the desert, in the course of which he conquered the Middle East. Similarly, I remember my father saying he was delighted when the Second World War broke out because it meant he would be away on active duty during the Northern Meeting Ball, and wouldn't have to go.

Everyone has a voice. Not all of us achieve it. Being inarticulate is not genetic. It is a failure of nerve. That is why we genuinely admire well-spoken people, by which I mean articulate rather than refined. They have achieved their eloquence either through persistence, curiosity, or the power of their heart – all expressions of courage. These people are prepared not only to face the truth but also to work it out. They are prepared to say no, to displease people, and to risk failure by experimenting. That is why in a group of people the dominant personalities are invariably the most articulate. After all, to express ourselves is one of the two reasons why we are put on this earth.

Listening to mothers berate their offspring is evidence of the fact that eloquence is a product of fearlessness. What a stream of invective! What oratory of criticism! What tremendous fluency when dealing with their children. Yet you can get the same women in a work placement or some alien social environment and you might not get a squeak out of them. If there is one person in the world a mother has power over it is her own child, and that freedom from frustration unleashes a torrent of words.

Love and knowledge have the same effect, as William Fletcher, author of a book on office politics called *Meetings Meetings*, notices when he wrote: 'Even the inarticulate will burst into eloquent oratory on issues about which they care fervently.' Similarly anyone emboldened by the spirit of the Lord as B. W. Maturin, author of *Some Principles and Practices of the Spiritual Life*, notices when he talks of, 'the power which unsealed the lips of the shy, reserved person.'

CHAPTER TEN

Parties

1 I DON'T WANT TO GO BUT WHERE'S MY INVITE?

I dread going to parties, but I love having been to them (mostly because it means one less party I have to go to in my life). Unfortunately, if there is one thing worse than having to go to a party, it is not being invited.

Why am I like this? Fear. Life is incredibly simple without fear, but you put that hollow head fuck into the equation and you are being pushed and pulled into all sorts of contradictory directions. Even so, I know people who genuinely love parties. They plan them, look forward to them, talk about them, go out and spend time and money dressing up for them, go to them, shine at them and tell you about everything you have missed if you have made your excuses and managed not to go to them.

2 CHIEFS DO NEED INDIANS

Parties are made for beautiful women and witty men. The rest of us are there to make up the numbers. Even in London, where you can fill a room with party royalty, the concentration of cool becomes too daunting for the amazing people really to enjoy themselves. The elite need the minnows. We really are important. Chiefs do need Indians.

There is also a third category of person who naturally enjoys parties. They are the simpletons. These people are tailor made for nothing serious: saying *how do you do* a lot; five minute chats; plenty of exclamation; looking happy; and then finally indulging in the most ridiculous activity I can imagine for grown up people.

Contemporary dance involves jumping up and down in a room. They do this on the TV show *Jackanory*, but also at Annabel's. It is like there has been no progress.

Disco dance asks you to act out the ridiculous notion that you are a sex god even though you might be a late middle-aged primary school teacher prone to asthma. You cannot afford to let the thinnest shaft of still light into a nightclub otherwise you might be rumbled. This is why, unlike the more sensible waltz where at least you get to hug your partner, modern dance is conducted in the dark with lights that whiz around the place in a now-you-see-me-and-now-mercifully-you-don't sort of way.

3 PARTIES ARE ENFORCED JOLLITY

What is it about parties that turn perfectly sensible people into blithering idiots? Sometimes I look at people in astonishment and feel like saying: 'Would you like to go and lie down somewhere and come back when you are feeling better? Or are you normally this banal?' And I am not much better myself. Sometimes I feel myself being so boring that I want to go to sleep. And yet in more conducive circumstances I can be quite interesting and amusing.

Why does your mind go blank at parties? The answer is the self can disappear beneath the onslaught of a lot of other selves. The self needs grounding to withstand the power of other selves. It needs earth, not air, and parties are a vacuum.

Part of the problem with parties is their enforced jollity. You get out of your car in a subdued state of mind, rather daunted at the prospect of the human tsunami about to engulf you the moment you step in, but you are expected to be immediately happy.

I mean, what is the statistical likelihood of 100 per cent of the people in the room being simultaneously happy. This is what Graham Greene writes about happiness: 'Point me out the happy man and I will point you out either egotism, selfishness, evil – or else an absolute ignorance.' In other words parties, which set happiness as a social norm, are the epitome of fake. That is why they are such a strain on the psyche.

A party is a jungle where it's dog eats dog. Nice gets you nowhere at a party. What with one thing and another, it is not surprising cocaine has become epidemic in society. It guarantees self-confidence. It breaks your own ice. It makes you feel invulnerable and it gives you one hell of a good kick if you get enough of it up your nose. The only drawback is it makes you pretty well incapable of listening to the other person. Alcohol, on the other hand, merely exaggerates you while reducing, but not eliminating, your ability to listen. Ears are funny things. They just don't respond well to artificial stimulants.

I would love to go to a party where nothing was expected of you. You could act as you pleased. In the initial stages I would feel most inclined to sit down with a newspaper, then once the drink had begun to take effect I might gradually start talking to somebody on the fringes of the action, before maybe launching myself into the general mêlée.

Parties are joy by design, but that is not how joy operates. In fact like everything emanating from the Second Self, joy is a perverse creature that often finds expression in the most unlikely of situations. I would definitely say none of my best conversations have happened at parties, despite the fact that hosts and hostesses go to great lengths to create an environment where the opportunity for happiness is maximised. One tip I would offer. Loneliness helps you enjoy a party. It also gets you out of the house. It propels you into other people's company. I have found since my marital separation that anything is better than staying at home alone – even parties.

4   PARTIES ARE THE MOST IMPORTANT THING IN YOUR LIFE

Be that as it may, parties are the most important thing in your life. Think about it. What activity is more important? Remember that the bible says all is vanity. So that puts pay to self-important writers and artists who have the audacity to prioritise their work. The greatest *oeuvre* in the world is ultimately a piece of entertainment, whether its medium is visual, aural or literary. Art is just a manipulation of that experience. In his letters to his brother, Van Gogh makes the point that art does not make you happy. Only life can do that.

The reason why everybody thinks they have got a book in them is because we have all got a story to tell and it is the one about our lives. There is a creative spirit in us all. Of course, the vast majority of us put the pen down almost immediately, but what we are still left with is our creative urge. The question then is what to do with it. The answer is to express it at a party. This is the place where you present yourself in your most attractive form. It is pertinent that the word 'art' is in the middle of the word 'party'. A party is a highly stylised art form. It is a formal, ritualised situation. Do not be taken in by casual dress codes. Even they themselves need to be meticulously obeyed. Whether it's black tie and tails or ripped T-shirts and wearing your jeans lower than your underpants makes no difference. You will obey. No one goes to a party without first thinking about what to wear. Like any other art form, the effect is pre-planned. Your aim is to look and sound natural, but it is all intentional.

5   NICE GETS YOU NOWHERE AT A PARTY

At a party, your aim is to be entertaining. You don't aim to be virtuous or industrious or prosperous. That is all irrelevant at a party. That is what you do in your work and domestic lives. This is a party and we want to see what art there is in you. Yes, it does matter how you dance. We want to see whether you can move with style and grace.

But most important of all, we want to hear how well you talk and how well you can listen to other people. Quite frankly, at a party it does not matter how successful you are in your career, it will not get you through the next conversation any better. I met a postie in the bar the other night and he was scintillating. His easy wit made me cumbersome despite my apparent achievements and my superior bank balance.

6   A PARTY IS THE ULTIMATE COMPARISON SITE

A party is the ultimate comparison site. It is the place where you can lose your wife to another man. She will see you in comparison with other men and woe betide you if you are found wanting. It is precisely how I lost my wife.

I was certainly more virtuous than the other three men she proceeded to have affairs with, but that was because I was the only one who was supposed to be having sex with her. That was an easy moral victory. I was more intelligent than two of them and I was richer than one of them. All three of them were bigger and better looking than me, but that is not why Sarah betrayed me. The real reason was that all three of them outperformed me at parties.

Female psychology was explained to me very simply by my sister, Arabella. She recalled her days as an average looking single young woman. She said that along with all the other girls, she used to fancy the coolest and most amusing young man at a party. She had to make do with people further down the pecking order, though, until she reached the level of her subsequent husband, Joshua. She says if you concentrate on somebody you can fall in love with them. Joshua took some effort but she got there in the end! You only have to look at nature to understand the way women behave. All the hinds make themselves available to the top stag.

7   HOW TO BE FUNNY

Wit is most prized at parties, but unlike beauty, the other quality around which people congregate at social gatherings, wit can be acquired. Yes, I think some people are born with a silver tongue. It's just in their DNA. Nevertheless school and home dictate the way you talk. Some people are fortunate enough to come from families with an amusing way of thinking and talking and they just fall into line.

School, like all communities, sets a premium on wit and mastery of the art is a route to popularity. So many professional comedians trace their career in humour back to a particular moment at school when they consciously made the decision to amuse their school fellows, either to avoid being bullied or to ingratiate themselves with the elite members of their peer group. It proves that wit can be copied, studied and acquired. It is never too late to learn or develop what wit and humour you already have. First you need to gain a sense of detachment. For the duration of the story, or just for the moment of comic response, you must lose all self-consciousness and give your entire spirit up to the moment of comedy.

Look at the great comics. It is all done on delivery. Tommy Cooper's script, for example, was pitiful. That was his daring. How close he got to the horns of the bull. He was like a matador of mirth, hardly moving, hardly saying anything while the bull, which in terms of humour is silence or nothingness, bore down upon him. Great comics, like very funny people in one's private life, can slow their delivery right down, sometimes allowing themselves pauses, gaps or even silences and it only serves to redouble your laughter. All it takes is a sideways glance, a flash of teeth, the curl of a lip, the arch of an eyebrow, and a story can energise a room.

To be British is to be funny. It's what we do. Our language with its juxtaposition of formal Latin and gutsy Anglo Saxon, is designed for it. Two of the most brilliant and far-reaching developments of the modern age in this country have been the liberation of women and the evolution of humour. Think back half a century and see how far we have progressed. We honestly thought *Carry On* movies were funny. We actually thought they were witty. Compare that rubbish to the amazing stuff being produced on our televisions now. No wonder today's teenagers in this country are so amusing.

But what can we do who come from a cruder age? How do we catch up with our children?

8   THE PYRAMID OF WIT

First you have to provide yourself with motivation. You have got to realise that women love wit and men worship it. Nothing has changed the way we judge one another since the seventeenth century when the celebrated satirist, social commentator and playwright, William Congreve wrote *The Way of the World* in which he described the real social hierarchy that existed independently of money and position.

The real way of the world puts the wittiest men at the top of the social pyramid. He inevitably gets the most enchanting women. Of course, wit is not an accident of birth like inherited wealth or beauty. The acquisition of it requires tremendous verbal skills allied to empathy for others and an acute social awareness.

The expression of wit in Congreve's day insisted on command of the language in the service of anecdote, repartee and innuendo. Congreve's observation was that the wittiest person in a group is the most powerful. Eventually the top woman succumbs to the wit of the top man and agrees to marry him on the condition that she can 'choose conversation only to my own taste and to have no obligation upon me to converse with wits that I don't like'.

What's at the heart of most people, or at least a lot of people, is a basic lack of interest in others. People pretend to be interested, so you get a lot of noise that sounds like laughter, but look at the eyes and you see they are not really amused at all. And you get a lot of feigned interest. We are such nice people, helping one another through the tedium of social intercourse. And then you get the people who are alive and they can galvanise an entire party of people. You want to be one of those marvellous people. You can be.

10   PRETEND LIKE A CHILD

Here are a couple of tips from Oscar Wilde, who was that rare thing – a funny man in the Victorian age. 'A little sincerity is a dangerous thing and a great deal of it is fatal,' he wrote. He also wrote: 'A man is least himself when he talks in his own person. Give him a mask and he will tell you the truth.'

Now take the scene in *Butch Cassidy and the Sundance Kid* when they are trying to get employment as security guards and the Sundance Kid has to prove his prowess with a pistol, but completely misses the target. They are about to be dismissed when the Sundance Kid asks whether he can move. Permission having been granted, he darts to one side, pistols flashing and suddenly his aim is pinpoint accurate as the tin can he is shooting at dances from one place to another as bullet after bullet makes it skip across the ground.

And I will finish with two other relevant points: one from a hilarious, plump Devonshire dumpling of a woman I once employed to make scones and another from the celebrated, contemporary, erudite, wit and novelist Will Self. Will Self says of inspiration, 'I just open a bottle of wine by myself at home, jam up against a corner of my sitting room and talk nonsense.' And my Devonshire scone maker agrees. She once told me that if she's bored: 'I just says any old thing that comes into my mind even it's nonsense, in fact especially if it's nonsense.'

Oscar Wilde's tip is to act, pretend, perform, invent, fabricate, quite frankly lie – anything but be yourself. The Sundance Kid has to move to hit his target. He needs to free himself up to be accurate. The scone-maker from Devon and Will Self liberate themselves by spontaneous verbal exercise. These are the apparently crazy ways in which you can access your Second Self, where dwells your vital spark. Repartee is too quick for thought, It comes from that magic place in your Second Self.

11 WIT IS A SUBSET OF GUTS

But there is one quality required above all others, without which wit will die frozen upon your lips. It is the virtue that underwrites all creativity. Without this spirit at the core of your being you are the walking dead, one of the many millions whose lives are merely mechanical existence. These are the bores. They can be high achievers or lowly functionaries. Their conversations are limited to exchanges of CVs, glib opinions, and self-serving psychobabble. Sometimes it is shocking to see how boring a person can be when others are so captivating.

What is the quality that determines your place in society? Guts. Freedom of speech, without which it is not possible to be entertaining let alone funny, is an act of courage – not caring what people think of you, a daring to offend and a daring to dig deep into yourself in front of other people.

What happens is that a massive gap opens up between those who dare and those who don't and so in later life you discover the world is divided into scintillating people and dull people with hardly anybody in between. It is as if you have either got it or you haven't, the working class and the aristocracy often have it because for different reasons they don't care. It is the prospect of money that makes you care. The working class don't care because they are never going to get it and the aristocracy don't care because they have already got it.

What about the rest of us? Is there any chance of redemption? Can you, for example, learn not to care in late middle age? Yes, there is a golden opportunity after your children have grown up and left home. You no longer need money. Use that moment to change. The mind is habit formed. Inside you there is a lot of pent up feeling. Let it out. How? With words. Practise those words until with private exercise and public use you become fluent in being you. Because by the time you are fifty, you know that nothing else matters.

Fight or flight. It takes guts to stand and fight, to engage rather than find an excuse to avoid sustained contact with other people. The Chinese find eloquence so important that foremost in their ritual of welcome to babies at one month old is a ceremony that involves the baby being kissed on the mouth by a live fish. This symbolises nature's bestowal of the gift of eloquence on the new human being.

In the more mundane world of primary school, where you make your first faltering steps in the social world, you almost immediately notice that the big and the brave boys dominate the talk. You notice that talk comes with personality and you may now wonder which comes first. Are some boys just born more articulate than others or is it that some boys have more courage than others? They are the first and foremost to broach silence. They take nothingness head on. They are not cowed by it or by any of the other boys competing for supremacy.

Why at secondary schools do the pretty girls love the bad boys? You need guts to be bad. You need guts to be rude to people, to get involved in fist fights and to take on authority. And inevitably the bad boys at the back of the classroom, who might do abysmally in exams, have the best *craic* and they command the playground, which is proof that it's personality, not brains, that gives you freedom of speech. They can out talk the swots and the scholars.

New York socialite Alec McKaig wrote of Scott Fitzgerald and his beautiful wife, Zelda, the toast of the jazz age: 'Moreover she and Fitz like only aristocrats who don't give a damn what the world thinks or clever bohemians who don't give a damn what the world thinks are the best of company.' To that list I would add the bad boys at school and later in life manual workers. These are, of course, sweeping generalisations but you get the feel and it is the feel that counts. Wit also comes from self possession which, in turn, is a product of courage. You have to have the guts to be truly yourself and the reward is self-possession, the old fashioned word for cool.

There was that scene in the French café when Dick Diver, the hero of Scott Fitzgerald's *Tender Is The Night*, declared to his friends that he was the only cool American in the world. 'Dick said no American men had any repose, except himself, and they were seeking an example to confront him with. Things looked black for them – not a man had come into the restaurant for ten minutes without raising his hand to his face.'

Socially, the challenge is not to bolt back into the familiar but to risk thinking in somebody else's company or even to invent stuff on the hoof. It is like learning to ride a bicycle. To begin with you need support, somebody else running along beside you to catch you when you begin to fall, but then comes the time when you start to make a few revolutions of the wheel wobbly but unaided. Yes, in the early stages there are a number of embarrassing accidents; then suddenly you get it and it is easy. In the field of wit, your props are your repertoire of funny stories, humorous comment and comic quotes, but what you are aiming for is to let it all go.

12   REPLY TO THE LAST THING SAID AND YOU'LL NEVER BE AT A LOSS

Infinite talk is creative and responsive. Finite talk is the process of using your memory bank of pre-conceived ideas and anecdotes. Actors who spend their working lives pretending to be other people are particularly prone to stage fright in their private lives. 'Actors are incapable of handling life's realities,' writes Lionel Jeffries in a story compilation called *Cheers!* collected by Phyllis Shindler. 'On stage, or in the studio, there is a total control but on Life's Stage – disaster! The slightest hiccup in the unrehearsed events of everyday existence throws them into a high state of anxiety. The general public take it as being grand.'

One of the main reasons adolescent conversation, for all its limitations in terms of knowledge and awareness and consideration, is so often more lively than ours is because teenagers have very little material in the memory bank to fall back on. Their references are in short supply so they are forced to use the present tense in their conversation and that leads to fun. It also tends to make them very accessible to one another. Conversely, the problem of social intercourse in later life is that people have such an extensive back catalogue of experience and information that conversation can lose its immediacy. It can degenerate into a huge exercise in explanation. Not having references in common is one of the drawbacks of no longer living in community.

13   SIX STEPS TO FREEDOM

Here are six tips that will help you to let go of yourself and your need to control conversation so that you can give yourself up to the *craic*:

1.   *Craic* is circular
2.   Reply to the last thing
3.   Exercise verbal foreplay
4.   Imagination is Latin for picture
5.   Speed up your texts
6.   Role play

If you forego your ego and enter a social circle like a rugby club, a public bar or a dinner party circuit, you may initially not feel up to speed with the merry banter, but if you stick around long enough you will begin to see a pattern to the humour. What's more, you will notice that it's the same old subjects being given the same old treatment time and again. If you find yourself not quite getting the rhythm and meter of the *craic*, you can practice at home with your journal, experimenting with trial replies. You might think such rehearsal too naff for words, but it is just a creative way of remembering people whom you have met. It is better than watching the telly. You don't know those people.

Craic is attitude turned into humour. Take my pub in Inverness, for example. The automatic role my customers and my staff insist on me playing – the stereotype from which they will not let me escape – is that of the idle, sex-starved, plutocratic, skinflint who exploits his hard working, brow-beaten staff. I, on the other hand, cast my staff in the role of skiving, irresponsible, pilfering chancers who are unemployable outside the four walls of my establishment and, but for the infinite goodness of my heart, destined for the dole heap. As for my customers they are bloody lucky they are not barred because they bring the tone down with their disreputable chat and poor dress sense. The *craic* is variations on those themes day in day out. On entering the pub you might think wit was quick if not slick. It would only take you half a dozen shifts to work out the patterns of exchange. Here's a smattering:

'Don't strain yourself, Kit. It's not like we need your help to serve all these people or anything!'

'Napoleon never pulled a trigger. I don't pull pints!'

'Yes, and the same goes for women!'

'What?'

'You don't pull them either!'

'Customers are our bread and butter not our bed and breakfast and one should always strive to keep it that way. As regards the female members of staff, I adhere to the cast iron rule that has served publicans well down the ages: Never shag the payroll!'

And then later I am cornered by one of my old regulars who is berating me about a 10p price rise on a pint of beer.

'You should be ashamed of yourself!'

'That goes without saying!'

'Your latest price hike. Don't think I've not noticed!'

'What 10p on a pint? It's nothing.'

'It might be nothing to you! You may well fart fivers for all I know but I have to eke a living out of the few pennies flung my way in the form of a pension from a grateful state and that extra 10p is breaking this camel's back!'

'O my heart bleeds!'

'I can take my custom elsewhere you know.'

'Is that a promise?'

'Ah you'd miss me once I'm gone!'

'I think my business could just about survive the loss of revenue I get from your pint and half. It's not as if you are one of my precious alcoholics!'

'You never know what will tip me over into alcoholism. Maybe your 10p price rise!'

The dialogue above is a classic example of role play. I am, of course, a very nice person who is immensely appreciative of his staff who, in turn, I think have a reasonably positive and affectionate attitude towards me, but where is the fun in the reality? How much *craic* would I get if I came in and said:

'Is everything OK? I hope you are not too tired from serving all those charming customers of ours.'

'No, it's fine. We get our fag breaks and time goes faster when you are busy. Don't trouble yourself on our behalf. You have got enough on your plate fending off the bank, the government and the council who between them take all your profits.'

Where is the fun in that? Role-play can be extended beyond your own personal situation to include any type of person in any conceivable situation. The world is your oyster. You can suddenly adopt the voice, body language and attitude of a depressed Mexican astronaut lost in space or a gay Texan traffic warden trapped between two cars or a vegetarian Greek God with a lisp turning his nose up at the sacrifice of yet another goat. Take your pick. There is a television programme called *Whose Line is it Anyway* where hugely gifted comedians act out scenarios of this sort made up by members of the audience.

It's easier to take off people you already know. Some people lend themselves to caricature and they are to be treasured. I had a gift of an uncle who recently died. He was an old fashioned English country gent straight out of P. G. Wodehouse. He lived in a massive mansion and with it came the patronage of the village church and despite being an agnostic if not atheist, he had to help the local bishop interview the new vicar whenever the sinecure became vacant. 'I never asked any religious questions,' he said to me once. 'I just used to ask them what school they went to and what they liked to drink!'

You get the flavour of the guy. He used to have a musical wallet that played 'Land of Hope and Glory' when you opened it. He said it was actually very useful because 'if you miss your back pocket, which is very easy thing to do late at night, you would notice because it would be on the floor being patriotic!'

He was a National Hunt starter. All he had to do was climb a ladder and shoot the starting gun six times a race meeting. 'Not that easy late in the afternoon if you have congratulated too many people in the winners' enclosure and on occasion retired to the bar!'

It is imaginatively liberating to be someone else for a while. Oscar Wilde is right. Don a mask on occasion. You should have half a dozen characters up your sleeve. When the Goons were all the rage, schools, colleges and universities up and down the country were fully of Neddy Seagoons and Bluebottles. Then came Monty Python, which juxtaposed extreme situation with characters who adopted the strangulated nasal tones of petty bureaucracy. That unleashed a million amateur ambassadors of Neasden and then the sarcastic and exasperated voice of Basil Fawlty rang throughout the land.

Conversation is a mental dance between two people expressed through the spoken word and like dance it comes in many different styles, moods and tones but the important thing is to be in step with your partner. Obviously what you don't want is one person hogging the limelight to the exclusion of the other person.

It is also like a game of tennis with the purpose of trying to keep the rallies going for as long as possible. The way to do that is to learn to reply to the last thing said and if your partner similarly responds, you will have arrived at the infinite. There is nothing to stop your conversation going on forever except your next appointment and that breeds a social ease and a happy lack of self-consciousness that comes from an enviable attention to the present in general and to what is actually being said to you in particular.

The only problem about conversation is that it happens too fast for you to think of a good reply or for you to get just the right words to do justice of what you want to say. I have often wondered why Jane Austen's characters were so incredibly well spoken. The answer is that Austen had all the time in the world to couch their thought in the measured and cultivated language of enlightenment.

There is one beautiful technological invention that has slowed everything down and allows us to pick and choose our words at leisure. Long live texting on the mobile phone! See how you are never stumped for a reply to a text message and see how you love hearing the ring tone of your phone as it alerts you to the reception of yet another text. You can dread meeting people in real life and you can try and avoid the phone, but everybody loves text.

Seeing how easily witty you can be in a dialogue of texts, you realise that it is not imagination, humour or verbal dexterity you lack, it is merely speed. All you have to do is accelerate. How do you say things you wished you had said at the time? Not to care is important, as already discussed. Not to care so desperately for other peoples' approval. In fact get yourself to care only about the *craic*.

Why do self help books advocate daily mantras like 'I'm bloody marvellous!' for people who suffer from low self esteem? The self-help industry is right. Self-confidence is a hell of a variable for a lot of people and better to have a temporary lift than no lift at all. What we are attempting to do in this book is to make self-confidence permanent by giving you freedom of expression. Learn to love the *craic* and don't waste acres of time plotting material advantage or letting your job devour your consciousness. Keep your mind free and fit and flexible for the real business in life, which is to have fun with your friends. Pursuit of money kills the *craic*. Sales formulae are acquired and repeated and endlessly refined and they take the place of the beautiful anarchy of chat.

Some people say only love matters. I will tell you a simple story that will prove that only words matter. The pretty daughter of a friend of mine went to university and made five fabulous female friends and they called themselves The Famous Five after Enyd Blyton because it was naff and therefore cool in a post modern ironic way and they had the time of their lives and were sworn friends. In her third year she fell in love and started having a relationship with a charming fellow who was not quite as faithful as he could have been with the result she became obsessive and consequently no longer the amusing carefree spirit she had been in her first two years at university. So, of course, her friends gradually dropped her and her boyfriend lost interest in her, even though he was the cause of her loss of form.

Love and friendship are just feelings. That is all they are. They are the fruit of successful conversation and when that goes into decline so do the feelings. If poor *craic* injures, silence is a killer. It destroys everything in its wake: business, friendships, marriages, partnerships – you name it.

There are three aspects of the mind: will, intellect and imagination. Imagination comes from the Latin word 'image' meaning 'picture'. It is actually a visual thing. You conjure up a scene in your mind's eye and then all you do is describe it and people are amazed. The imagination offers you a very effective counterbalance to the relentless rational world of the intellect and the huge power of your will driving you towards success, insisting obsessively on purpose. The imagination reminds you that there is a third dimension to reality: the material existence of things. The imagination gives you complete freedom to do what you like with the things of this world without you having to obey the laws of nature. In your imagination a cow can jump over the moon. Lewis Carroll's *Alice In Wonderland* was a treatise on this very subject. It explored the relationship between language, logic and imagination.

Lack of imagination is a very dangerous thing and accounts for all the awful things we do to one another. Fritzel, who locked up his daughter in his basement for twenty-four years, raped her 3,000 times and had seven children by her, expressed regret at his trial and said he had never realised how cruel he had been.

Empathy is the work of imagination. The three aspects of the mind are not will, intellect and love. Love is a by-product of imagination. That is how important imagination is. How do you think ugly, plain and ordinary people fall in love with one another? Without imagination the world's population would be a tenth of its size.

CHAPTER ELEVEN

Silence

1 SILENCE IS THE OTHER WORLD

It is very important to have a private life. By that I mean an inner life, a diary, an internal running commentary, books by the bedside, poetry in the lavatory, a daily prayer routine. Otherwise you will just be side-lined by other peoples' talk and telly.

'A man should keep for himself a little book shop, all his own, quite unadulterated, in which he establishes his true freedom and chief place of submission and solitude,' wrote France's great essayist Montaigne. Virginia Woolf wrote a book called *A Room of Your Own* arguing that was all you needed to achieve personal freedom.

2 HOW TO AVOID LETTING YOUR LIFE SLIP THROUGH YOUR FINGERS

Life can be divided into three compartments: people, ideas and art. I recommend buying three hardback lined A4-sized journals of different colours starting with a red one, which you use for private thoughts of your own, especially items of human observation and maybe your own speculations on the human condition. 'The unexamined life,' says Socrates, 'is not worth living.' So examine it.

This is your own personal philosophy book, full of your own homespun theories: the fruit of your reading, thinking, watching, listening and experiencing. Yes, use it as a quote book as well – anything that catches your fancy. I use the right hand pages for my ruminations and the left hand page for what other people say or write about life, God, women, sport, nature, language, meaning, everything. And I number each item. Over ten years I have written seven hundred points about talk, which have given birth to this book.

The second hardback book should be blue and indexed A to Z. This book should be your people book. You should list your friends and relations and devote a page to each one. Supposing you have a friend called Jane, you flip to the letter J in your index and you jot down your diary entry about her – something she has said or done that has caught your imagination – on her page. And number the entry. I number everything. It is cool to be able to say to yourself: there are twenty-three things about Jane that have amused and interested me. Without a journal to remind you, you would with the passing of time probably only remember three of them.

The blue book is your most important journal because whereas your arts diary and your philosophy diary may make you more interesting as a person, your people diary gives you closer connection to members of your social circle. Friendship flourishes only if you concentrate on it and there is no better way than hoarding details about the people you have specially chosen to record in your journal. I think it is shocking the way people know more about the lives of characters on a tri-weekly TV soap opera than their own friends let alone neighbours.

Psychobabble is how we dissect one another with analysis. Fine as far as it goes, but not the point of your blue book, which is to enjoy other people. It is not psychic health that necessarily recommends other people to us. It is their *craic*. The point of the blue book, like prayer, is to immerse yourself in other people by thinking about them in detail and taking a delight in their idiosyncrasies and their essential uniqueness and the best method is just listing their doings and sayings.

I will take one page out of my blue indexed people journal to show you the sort of items I collect about people precious to me. Chris Swift is my neighbour, a hard working middle-aged farmer: fit as fuck and hands like shovels. He spent his early days roughing it in Africa. He does not read the Guardian.

1. Swiftie says he gave up smoking in 1980 the day Mugabe came to power.
2. 'Peter Hain screwed up my plans for seeing the Springbok tour by putting tik tak on the road and generally making a nuisance of himself,' he says referring to Peter Hain's activities as a student. 'He is now the foreign affairs minister for Africa.'
3. Compares Western influence in Africa like coming here in the Middle Ages and offering helicopter gunships and machine guns to Highland chiefs. Absolute mayhem.
4. Recollection of me reading poetry at West Coast tenting weekend. 'Oh yes you started reading Bates to us.' 'No, Swiftie, the name is Yeats and he's the most famous poet of all time!'
5. His heroes are all action men like the intrepid Antarctic explorer Shackleton and Cecil Rhodes' sidekick, Saloux about both of whom he has read extensively, otherwise he does not touch books. The things he takes seriously are corncrakes and red kites and how to attract them on to his farm.
6. Likes the idea of drinking wine out of two glasses keeping one in reserve so you are never empty.
7. His secret to getting the decision right about when to cut his hay. 'Skilful mismanagement!'
8. 'The advantage of being narrow-minded is that anything within your field of vision is actually noticed, properly examined.'
9. 'I can drink beer at lunchtime because it just sloshes around in my brain in the afternoon but as I don't have to use it at all in my work, it doesn't matter.'
10. One of his favourite expressions: 'Show the dog the rabbit!'

The third journal is black and should be devoted to cultural comment: what you and other people think about books, plays, bands, TV and films *et cetera*. And if you are interested in politics, politics. How many books have you read and really enjoyed and yet a year later you can barely remember the book's title, let alone the plot or the reasons you loved it so much and what you learnt from it?

3   CULTURE SHOULD BE DIGESTED

Whatever your monthly consumption of culture, each item that impresses you should become part of you. In a month I probably read two books, see ten TV films and two films at the cinema. That is only fourteen cultural items. They will all be noteworthy or else I would not have decided to read or watch them in the first place. I should want to treasure the best bits in my memory bank. I should want to articulate my appreciation of them. Remember self-expression is half the point of life. It is feeling that fuels words and the effect of art is to stimulate feeling in you.

There are two reasons you need your black diary. There is not always the right person at the right time in the right place for you to pour out your feelings about a work of art you have just experienced and secondly, until you have learnt the language of cultural analysis and appreciation, it can be frustrating trying to explain your love of a book or film. A diary is a great place for self-education. You can build up your vocabulary, collect the words of analysis appropriate to the genre of art under review. There will only be about five hundred of them. And then you can experiment cultural comment without the ferocious time pressure imposed on you by the immediacy of conversation. You can ask yourself what you really think of a piece and then take time to go find the right words. You do that privately you will become fluent.

4   SCHOOL IS A PARROT FACTORY

Via the Tricolour Diary System, this book recommends further education, even further than university because all forms of standard education are parrot factories. There is no difference in the style and content of essay questions set at A level as at degree level and, what is more, you are only given the same ludicrously short period of time to give your essay answers. Degrees are just like A levels. They are memory and speed tests – the most rudimentary methods of assessing intelligence and certainly providing no incentive to the genuine acquisition of knowledge.

School and university education is designed to make you know a little about a lot. That is the very opposite to what is being proposed in this book. Most people's real education starts after they have left their *alma mater* and they have started to think for themselves. I am catering for them.

Conventional education for most people is experienced as a blur, a background noise which, when it does work, operates by osmosis. Sometimes the individual kicks in but mostly you end up with a fluent parrot. It makes you employable, amenable to the acquisition of the next language you need to learn: that of your chosen career. Real thought occurs only when you actually come to practice your profession and is so often only restricted to that field of activity. So you get that sinking feeling with so many people who are interesting only about their work. Otherwise they are so much dead meat. The point about the black diary is to make you interesting about culture. The red diary is about your life and the blue diary is about other people.

'In prayer we shall reap the fruits of the carelessness or watchfulness of an ordinary life,' writes B. W. Maturin in *Some Principles and Practices of Spiritual Life*. Whether you believe in God or not, you can learn a lot from priests, gurus and spiritual leaders because they spend their lives thinking about how best to live. In his quote

Maturin is emphasising the cultural importance of the need to be watchful in your life. Diary keeping is a form of keeping watch. Real journal junkies are avid collectors of life. They are as alert and watchful as bird spotters. My family motto is simply *Je suis Prêt*, which means 'I am Ready' or 'I am Alert'.

The perfect conversationalist plunders his education to enhance his talk so that it is free to roam beyond the here and now. His quality of individual thought informs a fluent and singularly accurate use of language serving a happy interplay of wit and insight. His, or in this case her, manner of speech is described by Margaret Drabble in *The Radiant Way*, a book about women who have come into the fullness of their being. 'She understood the art of conversation, she did not leap or grasp obsessively or take too great, too sudden, too idiosyncratic an interest in a subject, she understood the importance of a bright, smooth, easy, transitional manner.'

5 YOU ARE THE HEADMASTER NOW

How to attain that ideal? Well, the great thing about the diary method of further education is that the lunatic is in charge of the asylum. That is you and your mind. This whole book is about expressing yourself. It is very much anti-parrot. Kill that squawking bird.

We believe in the individual within the group. The problem is that most people are groupies, which is why they worship stars: unreal images of amazing people. As Christ himself said: 'All men are sheep.' Well, not quite all because we are bucking the trend here with our Tricolour Diary System.

In your black journal you are not being subjected to subject matter determined by an absent professor. You pursue the things that interest you, be it the film you have just seen or the book you have just finished, a newspaper article that has caught your fancy or some crazy thing on the telly. This is the organic way of learning.

It is the way in which my brother Rory came to know – as in real knowledge not parrot speak – more about art than anybody I've met this side of the TV screen. In his early twenties Rory was suffering in the city as a pinstripe monkey earning a pittance (those were the penal days before Big Bang that led to Credit Crunch). To cheer him up and give him some relief from the treadmill, my father gave him a present of £1,000 to spend on paintings. My father had noticed a little green shoot of artistic interest in his son.

Dreading to squander a penny of his windfall, Rory spent his lunch hours tramping round the galleries of London looking and looking at art for sale. He started to get his eye in. He also read voraciously. Then he began actually to part with money and acquire some paintings. Thirty years later he took early retirement from a career as an estate agent, then money broker and finally arbitrage trader, to exchange his city suit for an artist's smock. And at the age of fifty, having by then built up quite a collection of paintings valued at over £100,000, this man with no discernible artistic talent took up painting himself.

Because of his wealth of knowledge, within five years he had become a recognised artist himself, exhibiting and selling his paintings for over a grand each. 'It's not talent that matters, I don't have any,' he explains. And he is right. Of us four brothers who went to a prep school called Moreton Hall in Suffolk, he was the only brother who did not get the art prize (which was really a consolation prize for boys who were not quite clever enough to be in amongst the academic prizes but had enough hand eye co-ordination to hold a paintbrush and vaguely waggle it in the right direction).

'It's attitude and knowledge that counts and the guts not to endlessly repeat yourself once you have brought something off,' he says.

The reason I use Rory as a fine example of self-education is that he could have gone to art school and become a parrot. Instead he thought for himself, and his learning curve was of his own making.

As noted before, the two main impulses of man in pursuit of self-fulfilment are love and knowledge. The point of the indexed blue journal in which you are enumerating, describing, recording and quoting from family, friends and acquaintances is to make you grow in affection for them. The more you know about a person, the more you are aware of them, the more you appreciate them and that is just one short step from love.

Realisation is another word for knowledge. It is what is happening to a person when they say: 'Oh, I see!' or 'Ah the penny's dropped!' From your red journal where you enumerate and record your observations, insights and perceptions, you will find that knowledge grows as one realised truth leads to another in an endless progression earning you the gradual emergence of an expanding consciousness.

Apart from improving your conversation and your ability to connect with other people, this material you have garnered from your life might actually have some practical use for you. Take top pop lyricist, Paul Heaton's testimony:

> My lyric writing came from a form of hoarding, without a doubt. At school I kept exercise books full of conversation between me and my mate, which we passed to each other while the teacher wasn't watching. I've still got things like that. I've still got quotes from when I was working in an office, if anybody said anything daft. And still, if I think of something, I make myself write it down.

6   DON'T JUST WRITE YOUR DIARY. READ IT.

It appears to be a silly thing to say but you should periodically read your diaries. A lot of people keep diaries but very few people read them. A diary is a waste of time unless you read it. I am a particularly bad offender. I have religiously kept diaries for thirty years and I only started to read them to prepare for this book. I delved into my red journals and sifted through the seven hundred points I had collected about language. That got me curious about my other diaries and so I read them too and I was amazed how much of my life I had forgotten. It has been a revelation. The effect of ploughing through the million or so words I have written in my blue, black and red diaries has been to put a stop to my life of permanent postponement and make me address the key issues of my life which, like with everybody else's, concern the use of language in relation to other people.

The experience has made me take my own medicine. It has made me prioritise words. And I feel myself growing in leaps and bounds. I am gaining freedom through power. The lesson to be learnt here is that endless theorising does not make a jolt of difference. What makes you grow as a person is action. Instead of repetitive debate about what one should do, one should just do it.

7 HOW TO IMPROVE YOUR BRAINPOWER?

The mind is an ocean liner. It takes a hell of a lot to get it to change course. It steams along in whatever direction it happens to be going, even if it is in the wrong bloody ocean. It goes round and round in circles, sometimes like a cyclone when you're in the grip of an obsession, or sometimes like an idle glider in a gentle tail spin.

There are three things you can do with this cyclical energy. You can either consciously get yourself to direct your mind on to a subject, any subject in the world, and get it to feed on it. Or you can increase the size of its cycle. That is the effect of enlightenment or enlargement of self.

Some people's minds go round in ever decreasing circles until they end up in old age as scared little rabbits down their little bolt holes, rarely coming up for air. The bigger the person the greater the circle. So you occasionally come across amazing people, like Zorba the Greek, who has never read a book in his life, knows nothing about the arts and cares not a fig about politics, but whose powerful circular mind can extract every ounce of experience out of any encounter that comes his way. The author, Nikos Kazantzaki, uses his narrator to express a writer's admiration for a man of the moment: 'I weighed Zorba's words – they were rich in meaning and had a warm earthy smell. You felt they came up from the depths of his being and they still had a human warmth. My words were made of paper. They came down from my head, scarcely splashed by a spot of blood.' For blood read life.

Haven't you come across people like Zorba? Normally found in the working class. No erudition but they can make the simplest utterance sound powerful because they have mixed it with experience. The point is there's more direct action (reality) in digging a ditch than in a hundred persuasive phone calls: what passes for work in the city of London.

Don't be fooled by the money and the status that goes with the 'work' of a pinstripe monkey! Work is what man does during the day and you can tell about the real worth of his work by the way he talks. Connection empowers talk. Zorba is a copper miner who works with a pick and he talks from 'the depths of his being' as deep as a mine. We all know what an estate agent sounds like.

The third thing you can do with your mind is open it up like the bonnet of a car and you can try and repair the engine. Here I am advocating therapy, education and prayer – three attempts at improvement.

Perhaps a better analogy is to see your mind as a transistor with a hundred billion crisscrossing wires. Your directing self is the soldering iron with which you can consciously make connections in your head. Every thought, word and deed makes a connection in your mind, which is why you can never truly break free of your childhood. Once a connection is made in your mind it is there forever. Sin is a bad connection. There may well be forgiveness, but there is no way of eradicating it.

Indeed one sin (the secular word would be inappropriate action) makes another more likely because the current of brainpower will now always have that option. There will always be that site available to be visited in those circumstances of thought. I see this in my pub:

once a pilferer always a pilferer. It is exhausting having permanently to instruct yourself not to nick. The thought does not even occur to a non-nicker.

The brain comprises of billions of microscopic cells called neurons which are biological signalling mechanisms. In other words, your mind is a billion signals. Green is a signal. Hill is a signal. Anger is a signal. Everything is a bloody signal. So the whole universe is in your nut. It is your life's work to individually activate as much of the universe as possible in your head. In fact by articulation – the process of activation – the putting into words that follows closely on the heels of, or sometimes even at the same time as experience, you make your own world.

Sartre overstated the case when he said the world does not exist except in your mind. In fact your experience of the world, which is the result of how you have processed information coming into your brain through your senses, is the world. I know that sounds like a tautology but what I am trying to say is that the world only has meaning according to how you interpret it. All the signals in the universe are replicated inside your head. It is how you marry them up with your experience of them that will determine the working of your mind. That is why the truth is so important. If you are deluded, you will malfunction and this comes out in various states of neurosis. Honour your neurons.

Neurons are organised into assemblies that have evolved to carry out certain functions. Each neuron consists of 20,000 synapses which are basically tiny gaps or channels through which exchanges of chemical signals take place from synapses of other neurons. Incidentally, neurons most often communicate with their neighbours in their communities but there is nothing to stop them communicating with complete foreigners. Alternative stand-up comics do that all the time and that is how they surprise us with their humour.

The brain works by electrical transmissions, which release chemical messengers that transmit signals from one neuron to another via their synapses. So your brain is powered by electricity that works on chemistry. It actually produces enough electrical energy to power a ten watt light bulb.

There is a walnut called the cerebral cortex which is responsible for language and a peanut called the hippocampus, which is your memory – two very important assemblies of neurons.

8 WAYS TO STRENGTHEN THE WORD / THOUGHT CONNECTION

The cerebral marriage you should be striving for is between thought and word. You want to work on accurate or effective signalling between the neurons in your cerebral cortex and all the other synapses in your brain. And I would recommend regular visits to the hippocampus. Memory is key to the training of the mind. It allows progress. Hence the importance of your three coloured journals.

Here are some exercises to help you strengthen connection between thought and word. The inspiration here is a comment I came across in a book by Rose Tremain called *The Way I Found Her*. She writes: 'Never play a game once; play it a second time. That way, your defeats are never wasted.' Be interested in those times when you fail in conversation to do justice to what you had thought. Go back during downtime and rehash that thought, take time to find the right words.

What you are doing there is repair work to the machinery of your mind. It is very important work. You are making accurate connections between neurons. Something physically actually changes in your head. You will feel your mind thawing – a constriction relaxing. That is not a figure of speech. I mean it literally. It feels like a dentist's anaesthetic wearing off. The brain, you see, is physical and it does give off physical feeling. When it is being sorely abused, you get a headache. Conversely, when it is being beautifully managed by just the right treatment – for example, the exercises I am recommending – you will feel what I can only describe as a mild thawing sensation, a relaxation, an ease. It is part of the reason why people who have command of the language and enjoy freedom of speech are so effortlessly relaxed.   ——

You do this enough times and you will see yourself becoming more articulate. Politics is primarily about repetition. A politician finds himself saying the same thing to journalists, constituents and fellow activists on a variety of different subjects and naturally what happens is they gradually become incredibly fluent. Just watch Question Time on television and you will see how much better a politician talks compared to a writer or a thinker who strive in their work NOT to repeat themselves. So they don't perfect what they say. They just chisel away at the written word and once it is committed to paper they rarely go back. Their quality of thought might be superior but not their articulation in the spoken form – which is what we are really interested in here because loving your neighbour and getting him or her to love you is not done through letters. A pen pal is not a real friend. Revisit a conversation where you have come off second best or where you have been stumped for a reply. It is actually good fun coming up with witty ripostes even if it is after the event.

As I have said before, the reason you and I are not as scintillating as the wittiest guy in our social circle is guts. It is not that we have inferior minds or that we were not born with the gift of the gab, it is that we simply dare not speak from our Second Self. We dare not let go and give in to our true selves, which is located in the font of our self expression from which energy force gushes a fountain of words and a brilliant spray of wit.

Here is the proof. I have seen schoolboy kings lose their way in later life. They have become tortured tortoises and dull rabbits, bewildered and tamed by the circumstances of their adult life, over-whelmed by the system. On the other hand, time and again have

I seen tentative teenagers and anxious young men gain strength through trial and error, growing into their glory in their forties and fifties.

How do they do it? Do you want it in a sentence? They react to failure positively. They do not allow their admiration for people better than them to degenerate into envy. Instead they learn the secrets of their social success by copying them before branching off and acquiring a style of their own. We often see people blossom at school and university, but what people often fail to appreciate is that the rate of growth and the possibility of change is just as radical in later life. Ernest Hemingway transformed himself at the age of forty because it took him till then to dare to uncover his true nature. That is why he made such a thing in his writing about courage because, of course, he was keenly aware of his own essential timidity. It took Gauguin until his late forties to give up respectability and security to dare to become himself. He ended up half naked knocking off masterpieces using a garish palate in a South Sea Bubble surrounded by mermaids. Previously he had been a pinstripe monkey.

Are we going to rise to the challenge or not? Most people do not, with the result that they are condemned to a life of increasing frustration and compromise. They become endlessly repetitive bores in old age. These people will have resigned themselves to the easy life of a parrot, preferring to talk in convention and formula, effortlessly and fluently delivered rather than to drum up the energy to think and talk for themselves.

Incidentally, people either think better than they talk or talk better than they think. Of course, one affects the other and you should consciously try and improve both faculties if you want to maximise your life.

On the other hand, there is a gutsy minority who do rise to their mid-life challenge and who in the most profound essence of their being say unto themselves with biblical solemnity: 'I am what I am and I will say what I think.'

9   HOW TO BECOME MORE ARTICULATE

This book assumes you have already said that to yourself – otherwise you would not have bought it in the first place. The point of this book is to nourish your courage with argument and illustration and to show you ways in which you can learn to say what you want. It lays down various principles about the relationship between thought and words allowing you to apply them to your own unique out-look. I offer you exercises, horribly self-conscious-making and deeply cringe-worthy though they might be, but nevertheless don't think learning to play a musical instrument is particularly glamorous. It is just as painstaking. And what awful squeaks and squawks are heard during the hours, days, weeks and months before we are treated to beautiful melodies!

They say it takes 3,000 hours of practice and study to master either a musical instrument or a foreign language. Well, surprise, surprise: that is all it takes to learn your own language, the language of your own true self in response to the many ways of thinking and talking you come across in your social and cultural life. Obviously I am not advocating the cranky idiosyncrasy of somebody withdrawn from other people, lost up his own arse. I recommend one hour a day for 3,000 days – that is ten years. Or double the daily dose and halve the decade.

Wit is the product of the interplay, with the emphasis on the second half of that word, between your brain, your heart and your guts. Further proof that wit is not inherent is that when you have enough time to yourself and you are not daunted by the presence of other perhaps more dominant personalities and you actually concentrate, you can surprise yourself with the facility of your mind. A classic case of this is the mobile phone. See how witty you can be in a text.

Crude though it might be, what I recommend is revisiting con-versations and improving on them in the privacy of your own study by coming up with better replies. You do this a few times and you will be amazed at how polished has become your patter and you are well prepared for the next encounter bearing in mind that most *craic* is cyclical. It's the same types of jokes and quips coming back time and again with the same people. Horses for courses, jokes for blokes.

Watch people when they talk and you will notice that certain people never leave their comfort zone: the talk is not only about their pet subjects – primarily themselves, their work and their world – but also the style of chat is complacent and self congratulatory and they never depart from their script: the product of what they have experienced through their five senses.

Then you get other people who are keen to make up stuff, embellish a story, pursue a line of thought, and accompany you on some absurd conceit. Quite frankly, they feed their curiosity and use their imagination. These people normally ask lots of questions and are attentive, responsive listeners with the result that their talk is infinite. They are our role models. There will be some people of this type in your social circle. Copy them.

Teenagers who hang about in groups doing nothing much but chat are very often highly accomplished at taking part in communal banter. Sadly they go on to enter the white collar world of work and often lose this marvellous facility. Then in later life have to take conscious steps to regain it. Hence this book.

Obviously I am not saying you shouldn't tell funny stories about things that have happened to you or that you shouldn't trot out well considered opinion, formulated through previous discussion and private thought. But I do think that you should jump at the chance of being led in conversation by somebody else, and actually inventing stuff on the hoof that has not occurred to you before. We love it when comedians improvise on stage. We are amazed by it and yet we should be doing it all the time in our social lives. This is a new habit you should inculcate and in private practice. It is truly liberating. The world divides into two. Those who do (who have all the fun) and those who don't (who don't). Repetition can perfect but it cannot compare with the power of originality.

> Thus has he – and many more of the same bevy that I know the drossy age dotes on – only got the tune of the time and, out of an habit of encounter, a kind of yeasty collection, which carries them through and through the most fanned and winnowed opinions; and do but blow them to their trial, the bubbles are out.
>
> *Hamlet*, 5, 2

Exchange of opinion does constitute an active but minority part of our conversation. Better that it is genuinely of your own making so that you are fully engaged in the exercise, than doing the mental equivalent of what Hamlet calls blowing bubbles. Make your own 'yeasty collection' of opinion if you must, in the privacy of your journals, which at least can afford you the time and space to think for yourself. Incidentally, you will find yourself mentally equipped through self-imposed habit to think without prejudice in the company of others and that is the stage at which you can in all honesty call yourself an intellectual.

Watch *Question Time* to see how current affairs should be discussed and watch *The Late Night Review* to see how culture should be discussed. Television can call on the services of the finest minds in the country. It is worth tuning in to see how it is done in the highest echelons. You learn by example. The principles of debate are simple. The art, the skill and the power reside in its practice.

People on *Question Time* make one point at a time. They try to articulate it as concisely as they can with rhetorical effect (that's the art bit of articulate). Then they may attempt to qualify it. Then you will see them try and find an example to illustrate the point they are making. They also search for incontrovertible evidence in support of their point. Observation, explanation, illustration. Try it yourself. Remember, one point at a time.

Another very good exercise is to read a newspaper opinion piece that catches your fancy and then try and repeat it yourself. Then repeat the exercise noting the vocabulary used and the sentence construction until such time as you have got it yourself. Note to self: there is no place for pride in self-education. You might dread any of your friends even imagining that you are spending your leisure time memorising other people's opinions but just remind yourself that you prefer to sacrifice cool to being tongue-tied. Don't think Barack Obama does not practice in front of the mirror! And the end result will not be to make a parrot of you because the second stage of the exercise is to make the style and content, the word and meaning of the piece, your own. You will have so familiarised your thoughts on the subject that you will find your own mind kicking in with its own reactions.

In the initial stages of self-education don't be too proud to copy. After all, the old masters of art used to do that. It was the way in which they learnt how to paint. So if it is good enough for Rubens, it's good enough for you. There is a scene in *Women in Love* when Hermione comes across Birkin making a copy of a Chinese drawing of geese. 'But why do you copy it? Why not do something original?' Hermoine says. Birkin replies: 'I want to know it. One gets more of China copying this picture than reading all the books.' And it is amazing what you discover when you really concentrate on a thing.

There is no more successful student of language than a child just out of his nappies. The most gifted linguist in the world cannot compete. An under-five learns the rudiments of the language in about as much time as it takes for him to learn to poo in a pot. What is the secret of his success? Slavish imitation and total concentration. The little nipper copies everything that moves: words, tone, idiom, manner, inflection, phraseology, slang, dialect, humour, accent. You name it, they just copy it and in three years flat they speak like a native.

How can we adults compete? Just copy them. We have so much to learn from children:

Positive competitiveness
Talking to yourself
Role play
Obsession with fairness
Total concentration
Love of play
Love of treats
Love of friends
Love of dressing up
Sense of excitement
Ability to laugh
Immediate responsiveness
Constant bickering
Delight

Because their egos are so undeveloped, they give themselves up entirely to whatever is attracting their amazing attention. They have the automatic gift of concentration. Watch a four-year-old pick up and admire a bauble. It could be gold. Everything is gold to them. How often have you see a toddler at a Christmas tree more fascinated by the Christmas wrapper than the present you have especially bought for them.

Zorba the Greek gets some good advice from the narrator about the power of concentration:

'You have seen what happens when you hold a glass out to the sun and concentrate all the rays onto one spot, Zorba? That spot soon catches fire, doesn't it? Why? Because the sun's power has not been dispersed but concentrated on that one spot. It is the same with men's minds. You do miracles, if you concentrate your mind on one thing and only one. Do you understand, Zorba?'

Zorba was breathing heavily. For a moment he shook himself as though he wanted to run away, but he controlled himself.

'Go on,' he grunted, in a strangled voice.

One good tip I have is to savour real life discussion, argument or even rows. They are invaluable for activating the mind. They provide you in the immediate aftermath with a charge of emotional energy to convert thought into word and say all the things that you feel you should have said and failed to say well enough. Use that energy.

What you should do is regard the initial disagreement that has naturally cropped up in conversation as Round One. Two things always happen in Round One. The better talker beats the better thinker and nobody's position changes one jot.

But now you go away and prepare for Round Two. You quietly consider the points made by your adversary and the only way to do that successfully is to set yourself the task of arguing his point of view. The other thing you have got to do is to beef up your vocab.

What you will have found in Round One is the frustration of not being able to articulate your argument accurately, swiftly or freely enough. Use Roget's *Thesaurus*, a mine of synonyms; dig up relevant literary or media text; and use what's already in your head. The words will be in there somewhere, just bring them to the surface of your mind. Hone your argument, assemble your vocab and go back into battle, and you will wipe the floor in Round Two. Never fails.

I recommend an invitation to re-engage along the lines of: 'I have been thinking about what you have been saying and I can see some validity in the points that you have made such as ABC but nevertheless ... ' Then you steam ahead and blind him with progress. Educationally a real argument is a gift as long as it is used profitably.

10 ARGUMENT FOR PRIVATE STUDY

They say that with life you don't get a second crack of the whip. I disagree. I think you do because I happen to believe in reincarnation, which explains the well documented phenomenon of *déjà vu* as well as well-documented incidents of regression under hypnosis where people without prior knowledge describe scenes of detailed historic accuracy. It also explains the Christian notion of purgatory. If you are just average to middling in your behaviour in this life, then you are sent to a place called Purgatory in the next. Well, don't tell me Purgatory does not perfectly describe life on earth. Yeah, I'm a bit of a Buddhist when it comes to the afterlife. I think you keep on coming back until you get it right, like Churchill who was held back at school for three years in his English class. End result: fantastic command of the language.

They also say life is not a rehearsal. I agree with this one and so does Shakespeare. The use of the word 'rehearsal' assumes by negation that what life is, by contrast, is a performance. That ultimately it is not natural. There is an art to it which you need to master to bring it off successfully. Shakespeare says the world is a stage.

If Shakespeare is right and life is a performance, you desperately need to rehearse for it. You do that in your downtime, which you should not fritter on TV and the internet. In fact if you are serious about transforming your life, I would advise skipping television during the week altogether and doing the socially unacceptable thing of going to bed early so that you have free time at the other end of the day, when you are fresh and full of energy before work.

Incidentally, one beneficial side effect of the Tricolour Diary System of Mind Training first thing in the morning is you arrive at work feeling relaxed, concentrated, energetic and playful rather than tired and rushed. Obviously, I totally believe in late nights with friends but you could reserve that for weekends. Balance is the key.

Your life only consists of days and not many of them: about 20,000 as an adult and each weekday probably only has two hours in it which you can all your own. I would start each day with half an hour of prayer (or similar) and one hour of what I call elocution: teaching yourself how to speak well. That is increasing your capacity for love and knowledge: the twin engines of life. And start the week by planning what exercises you are going to carry out in your five early mornings of study.

I am not saying that implementing the programme of self-improvement I recommend is easy. Especially in the early stages, it may well feel unnatural, pedestrian and laborious, although I guarantee you marvellous times too. All study has its rewards. But what I am saying is that for the poor old biodegradable slaves to the system that most of us are, that is the only route to freedom.

Do you ever feel you are not what you should be? Do you ever get glimpses of what you should be and what it feels like to be as you should? Do you ever get those feelings of lightness, power, energy and playfulness in you? That is what this programme will give you permanently. That's the prize. So it is worth the effort.

The alternative is a life of deep compromise. Are you one of those people beset with frustration because they can't say the things that they think? Or do you live in a semi-dormant state whose life has degenerated into a sort of mechanical triangular routine of work, telly, bed? We've all been there. 'Most people are only a very little alive,' was Baudelaire's famous dictum. The great Christian mystic, Thomas Merton, goes one step further: 'Most of the world is either asleep or dead.'

And what's more, I add, most don't even know they are making life difficult for themselves and others. Today's newspaper (November 5th 2008) reports on a survey which shows that 90 per cent of people at work in the UK feel bullied by their immediate superiors – and yet if you were to ask management whether they felt they abused their subordinates in this way, they would genuinely be astonished. Each and every one of them would imagine the report could not possibly be referring to him or her personally. Chronic lack of self-knowledge is the curse of ignorance that the Tricolour Diary System aims to lift.

If you actually write down what other people say and do and what other people think, you will become much more attentive to them. We are creatures of habit and natural born collectors. Every ten year old boy knows that. We must become habitual journal keepers. Yes, the pursuit of a better future desensitises us to one another. The purpose of the daily diary is to make us attentive to the present.

Progress is difficult to monitor where there are no qualifications or certificates awarded or indeed any marking system involving numbers to evaluate positive change. That is the problem of self-education. It doesn't go O level, A level, degree, Masters, PHD – because in real life progress is abstract. You have to judge for yourself. If you are on the right track, you will feel a growth in self-confidence, an improvement in the way you think and talk and you will find yourself getting on with other people better. Progress is not just gradual. Sometimes you get breakthroughs and you always get a honeymoon period at the beginning.

11   HOW TO READ A BOOK SO THAT YOU DON'T FORGET IT

We come from a literate society and yet most people don't know how to read. What they do is skim and promptly forget. How many times have you read a book and in two month's you can barely remember the title of the book, let alone the names of the main characters, the twists and turns of the plot, the best bits of the book, what it was really about and why you liked it so much? Most people read a book as if it is a race to get to the end.

Most experiences are rushed by contemporary people and this one is no exception. People even go on speed-reading courses so that they can say with pride that they are capable of reading a three hundred page novel at one sitting. It's like bolting food. Great literature is a mental feast. Don't treat it like a McDonald's hamburger. You should be enjoying it so much you should be dreading the last page. You should savour the stuff.

The greater the book, the slower you should read. *Brideshead Revisited* you should read at a snail's pace. Ditto *Bleak House, The Horse's Mouth, Mister Johnson, Tender is the Night, The Mosquito Coast, One Hundred Years of Solitude, Money, Zorba the Greek, Women in Love, The Unbearable Lightness of Being, Wind in the Willows, Gone with the Wind, The Grapes of Wrath, The Code of the Woosters, Catch 22, The History Man, A Prayer for Owen Meaney, Glittering Prizes, Madame Bovary, A Sunset Song, The Heart of the Matter, Captain Corelli's Mandolin* and *Birdsong*. My personal roll call.

You should treat your favourite books as your most treasured possessions. I have my top fifty books all in a row on a shelf in my bedroom. I read each of these books once every ten or twenty years of my life. So by now I have read them all two or three times and, of course, because they are works of genius, tremendous conveyors of art and wisdom, they tell me different things at different times in my life. You recognise and notice more and more as your deepening experience of life gradually opens you up to appreciate more and more of the masterpiece in your hands.

Remember the fundamental principle of knowledge. It is not the quantity of material consumed that educates a person. Even the most learned professor in the world can only have read the tiniest, infinitesimal speck of everything there is to read even on his or her own particular specialist subject. It is the quality of attentiveness that you bring to bear on the texts you come across in your life's enquiry that truly furnish your mind. The real question is how much of what you read do you make your own private possession. That is mental wealth. It's like visiting a house or owning it. Which counts as wealth?

I will tell you what well-read means. Best read means aloud, ideally to each other as they used to before the days of television. My mother read to my three brothers and myself *Under the Red Robe, The Four Feathers, The Children of the New Forest, The Scarlet Pimpernel, Flight of the Heron, Beau Geste* and the *Narnia* books – all sentimental romantic tosh, every one of them, but we were bewitched, cast under a spell of what we imagined were magical books. It taught me the power of the written word slowed right down to the speed of the spoken word and given expression and tone by a warm human being.

Well read is underlined, reread and contemplated.

Reading is a con. If it's a masterpiece you are getting the fruit of a genius' powerhouse of a mind expressed in his finest style at the outermost stretch of his abilities and the culmination of his entire being's experience of life turned into art at the scan of an eye and the turn of a page. It is a cheat and a shortcut. How do you absorb it into your being? If you realise it is far more important than anything else in your life at that given time, you will give it the necessary concentration that will allow you to take it into your being.

I imagine you think I am exaggerating about books. Libraries used to control the Middles Ages. The invention of the book enabled our civilisation. Before the book we were barbarians. Yes, we had song and dance but so does the aborigine and respect their culture though we might, it hardly compares with the Renaissance and what has subsequently ensued. Just one book made the West what it is today and another has made the East and a third has divided Europe and Asia and all three have created order and murder. Obviously I am talking about the Bible, the Koran and *Das Kapital.* So please don't tell me I'm exaggerating about the power of books. Films, music, dance and theatre are just side shows.

My friends and relations are very dear to me but they are babbling idiots compared to the geniuses whose works line my bookshelves. I listen to the sentiments and opinions of people I sit down to dinner with or stand up against the bar with, but the stuff they say is either crude convention or contradictory nonsense compared to the confounding truths and darting insights that are sitting there in printed form just waiting to be lifted off the page by my wandering eye.

Of course, there are a lot of crap books. In fact my personal experience is that there are very, very few books worth reading, but those few are mind blasters not only in what they say but the way they say it. These books are not only great aesthetic pleasure, they affect the way I think and so the way I actually behave. I am highly influenced by D. H. Lawrence, Joyce Carey, Jesus Christ, John O'Donohue, Evelyn Waugh, Ted Hughes, St Paul and Shakespeare.

Another reason why I read my top fifty books time and again is I have sent too many Booker prize winning books sailing through the air on the way to the bin not to want to avoid disappointment again. I fully understand Farve, Nancy Mitford's character in *Love in a Cold Climate* who only ever read one book in his life, *White Fang*, because in his opinion it was the best.

D. H. Lawrence said it was better to read just six books thoroughly in your life than inattentively hundreds of them. By read he means absorb.

I recommend reading a book with a biro. As you read, underline the lines you really like. To give you an idea of what to underline and why, here are ten underlinings I made in a great contemporary novel about adultery called *Who's Sorry Now?* by Howard Jacobson. I don't care what the literary critics think and I'm not boning up for an exam in English literature. I am just making the book my own, underlining the bits that appeal to me.

1. 'There never was a beautiful woman yet who didn't think her life had turned out less sensationally than her beauty merited.' I had never thought of that before and I'm sure it's true because beauty is a passport to any opportunity. Too much choice will

inevitably lead to disappointment because your imagination will plague you with alternative scenarios.

2. 'He had loved university, revered people whose profession were their minds, and missed hanging about, having time, talking over matters that need never be put to any practical or commercial test.' I love that summary of life at university, its privilege: the luxury of uselessness.

3. 'For him, no less than for Charlie, adultery was a disturbing concept and an adulteress a dangerously inflammatory personage.' Yes. Certain words carry huge associative power. Adulteress is one of those words. There is a naughtiness and a glamour to it.

4. 'I don't have to hush. Germans I can say what I like about. That's their function for the next thousand years – to be the butt of everyone who isn't German.' Nice bit of reverse racism from a Jew. Howard Jacobson is one of the tribe. I just think he must have enjoyed writing that line. Today anti-German is OK but not anti-semetic.

5. 'Kreitman was one of the generation that believed you had to sparkle conversationally, that you had to make wisdom fall from your lips like rubies while your eyes danced like showers of falling stars. You laboured at your coruscations and the woman was the reward.' Yes. You can win a woman with wit, as this book argues, but there are other aspects worth bringing into play like listening to the old bat.

6. 'The moral infection of nice had claimed him.' Yes, I am aware of the dangers of nice, as discussed elsewhere in this book.

7. 'For these were the great days of moral relativity, when whoever expressed a preference was a sermoniser.' I underline lines which better express what I think.

8. 'Every man was an Oliver Twist at heart, up for another helping whatever the dish.' A line about man's attitude to sex, I underlined it because I thought it was true, concise and funny.

9. 'Once it's asked, once it's seriously posed, it raises doubts and changes, ever so subtly, the balance of power.' It concerns various issues raised in this book. No two people are equally powerful and this is never more important to realise than in the context of a marriage which, for all the early high fallutin' declarations of everlasting love, is a power struggle. The person in charge can abuse their position so you do not want to make available any information, or admission, that can be used against you in times of conflict. The ideal marriage is one that is poised on an equal balance of power.

10. 'A conviction of the propriety of lightness, which Hazel secretly envied. Oh to be not very good at anything and see it as a virtue!' This is a sentiment close to the heart of the upper classes from whose ranks I am to be numbered . Never never to be serious socially is one of their mantras and excellence, the product of mastery of detail, is to be eschewed at all cost. Detail is dull, they think.

You see how different my appreciation of the book is from what you would expect from a university essay on the subject or a literary review in a newspaper? Not a bad thing considering Professor John Carey's view of modern literary criticism. He says: 'At a time when most literary criticism is, like alchemical love, deliberately made unintelligible except to a tiny band of initiates, and when the job-seeking young are forced to renounce common sense and their common language before they can gain employment in a university English department, Kermodes union of authority and clarity is redemptive.'

You will see from the extracts from *Who's Sorry Now* that I have noticed lines that address issues of power, language and performance. These are my current pre-occupations. They are actually the concerns of this book I'm writing and what rich pickings Howard Jacobson's novel has provided for me. His novel is primarily a study of the subject of sexual infidelity, but that does not stop me looking and finding these other things. The reader is half the story of a novel.

Having underlined a book and made it your own, you can then reread it any time in the future in about ten minutes – your underlinings will bring back the whole book to you in the way that it made sense to you. What I enjoy is when, say a decade later I have taken one of my favourite books down from its shelf and have decided to reread it line by line cover to cover, I turn the page and I see some underlinings. I know I am in for a particularly good time because there are greater lines ahead of me.

Having properly read a book you should be able to tell somebody else about it. It's one of the first signs of love. If you are madly in love with a woman, there is no greater enjoyment than telling your best friend all about her. Quite often talking about her is more fun than actually talking to her – which can be very hair-raising business involving the appalling risk of falling in her estimation by letting slip a remark or two a little less than scintillating. Similarly with a marvellous book you have just read or reread, you desperately want to tell people about it but you don't because you feel you don't have the linguistic ability. You just say: 'Oh, I've just finished a great book. You should get it. It's all about adultery. It's called *Who's Sorry Now?* by Harold Jacobson.' And then you might say something like: 'Apparently, although fidelity might be boring, adultery does not satisfy.'

Here is a five point plan on how to give your personal critique of a novel: how to tell your friend about a book.

1. Summarise the plot on one side of an A4 for your own benefit.
2. Ask yourself the key question: why did the writer write the book? What's he trying to get off his chest? What is he trying to prove? What is the point of the book? There is a book called *Sheltering Sky* that I found boring until I realised what it was all about. It is an investigation into the pursuit of happiness by

an intelligent couple liberated by money. How can a perceptive and calculating materialist with an equally privileged wife with all the means the world can offer him at his disposal, including travel of the world itself, find fulfilment? The inference being that but for the cash we are that person, but our lives our gobbled up by routine and duty.

3. What's the best bit of the novel? Re-enact the particular scene for the benefit of your friend. It gives him taster. It's like a film trailer.

4. Give him one juicy quote that you have memorised from the book.

5. Tell him why you loved the book which must include an explanation as to how the author has succeeded in carrying out his intentions for the book.

That's all. Not very difficult and you will find yourself saying more than: 'Get it. It's good.' This is what I would say about Howard Jacobson's *Who's Sorry Now* – 'He's even better than Nick Hornby who wrote *About a Boy* and *Fever Pitch,* both of which have been made into films. Jacobson has a fantastic Jewish sense of humour, a sort of sick fatalism about the folly of doing anything or even not doing anything. In today's world where everything is relative, what's the difference between vice and virtue if they both end in disillusionment.'

'The book compares the life of two equally dissatisfied middle-aged men: a faithful husband and a serial adulterer who eventually agree to swap wives. The faithful husband becomes very faithful to the friends' wife, but after awhile he begins to miss his original wife because of all they had shared over twenty years, so he eventually returns to her.'

'The adulterer takes to his opposite number like a duck to water. Corrupting a good woman is a novelty to him, for whom variety is the spice of life, but every new perversion including desecrating faithful wives has its life span. He ends up so degraded that only a trip to a professional dominatrix is perverted enough to give him the kicks to temporarily allay his essential loneliness. What the author seems to be trying to illustrate and so prove in his book is that both good and bad people are bad. It's just that bad people have the guts to be bad although badness is bad for you so you are better off trying to be good even if it is through fear or self-interest that you are making the attempt. Certainly, the chronic adulterer in the book is a far more attractive person than the erstwhile faithful husband even if he does come a cropper in the end.'

I would recommend the book for anybody contemplating adultery. Look before you leap. Peer into the abyss and *Who's Sorry Now?* will tell you what's in there. Furthermore, if women want to know what is going on in their husbands' minds, whether they are temporarily faithful or not, they need look no further than the pages of this book.

When offering an opinion, you don't have to be right. You just have to be alive. Here is a checklist of questions you should ask yourself of any book or film. Forget about plays. You hardly ever see them.

1. Do you identify with any of the main characters?
2. What's the point of the book?
3. Why did the author write the book?
4. Are you persuaded by the book?
5. Are the characters convincing?
6. What did you learn from the book you did not know before?
7. Did the plot keep you on tenterhooks?
8. What was the narrative hook?
9. What was the effect of the book – comic, tragic, poignant etc?
10. What emotions did it induce in you?
11. How effective was its literary style?

12. What was the moral dilemma?
13. What was your favourite scene?
14. How does the book compare with others of its type?
15. How good was the dialogue?

These are not the questions asked by modern literary critics but they are the questions asked by fellow writers and if they are good enough for them, they are good enough for us. It's the readers the writers have got to entertain not the critics.

12 VERBALISTICS

You have heard of aerobics, which is the business of putting your body through its paces in a series of exercises designed to optimise its fitness. Well, I recommend a mental fitness programme called Verbalistics whose purpose is a kind of frontal lobotomy. It's a way of making you mentally match fit. Here are some exercises.

1. Stereotyping is imagining typical people in typical situations. Imagine a typical scene taken from a book, a film or real life and describe it. If you don't have the words, go and find them and having made up the scene now animate it with characters and get them talking to one another in a way that is typical of them. Imagine, for example, a couple of ex-public school British subalterns playing chess together in a trench in the First World War.

2. Hyperbole and understatement. Apply both treatments to any story and you will familiarise yourself with the two comic staples.

3. Catchphrases and quotes. Collect them in your journal like a teenager does naturally. They make small talk, an albatross for many people, surprisingly good fun especially when you are stumped for a reply. A lot of these catchphrases have almost a universal application. 'I became famous for my 'repartee'. I

had a theory that there was one repartee effective for every situation and spent weeks in elaborating it. At that time the magic phrase seemed, 'Dear me, how very uninteresting!' If I had to choose one now it would be: 'This is a very bad moment for both of us.'

4. Take any subject and bombard it with questions and you will engender interest within yourself.

5. Belief and cynicism. Apply both responses to any subject. Argue both for and against.

6. Verbs. Collect and respect them because they enable sentences. They give them welly. Take a line from *Anam Cara*, for example. 'The sun brings forth the erotic charge of the curved earth.' In five minutes time try and repeat that line without first having consciously memorised it and you will recall the adjectives and nouns: the sun, the erotic charge, the curved earth but it's the verb makes the sentence possible but you won't remember it because it is just the facilitator. The sign of a good talker is his verbs. A charlatan just staggers from one noun to the next beefing them up with adjectives.

7. Very occasionally learn a poem or a song and repeat them to your self four times a year. After decade they will be second nature for you to enjoy when you are drunk like Zorba the Greek.

8. Verbal memory exercise. Choose a passage from a book or an article that you admire and perform the three-step *aide memoire*.

a. Read the passage, get the gist of the meaning and then attempt to repeat. Then go back to the original and see how weak your recollection is. You will also fully appreciate the author's use of language: choice of words and structure of sentence.

b. Now commit the passage to memory verbatim until you can repeat without mistake.

c. Now summarise the passage in your own words with your own thoughts. You will be aware of a novel ease and fluency in yourself, especially after that painstaking discipline of having so meticulously attended to the passage.

9. Summary. This is a diluted form of exercise of the above. Read a whole newspaper article you admire and summarise in your own words. If you find yourself stuck for vocabulary or ease of expression, borrow from the original. The ability to summarise: filleting a mass of information from its pertinent points is a skill much in demands in businessman and administrators. Most people can't see the wood for the trees and get bogged down in detail. Journalist Anthony Felix wrote of Dr Condoleezza Rice: 'It was her ability to break down complex issues to easily comprehensible tutorials that made her so prized at the Oval Office.'

10. Imagination. Write an endless shaggy dog story and keep it going for as long as possible and make it as silly as you want. Just liberate your mind from the shackles of experience. Let the little fellow off the leash. Start with the words: 'And there was this beautiful woman with a wooden leg … ' and off you hobble into the middle distance with idiot rubbish. My brother-in-law Joshua always has what he calls a book on the go, always has done since childhood. He just never gave up the practice of scribbling fiction with the result he has never lost the brilliant narrative imagination of the wonder of story with which all children are blessed. You can regain the attitude by taking up this creative practice. Joshua is the only person I know who truly writes for himself without a thought of publication. It's just fun. But it has transformed his *craic*, which is full of flights of fancy and hilarious non-sequiturs and graphic scenes of glorious stereotype.

11. Sticklers and sweepers. Adopt both attitudes to any given personal problem. I personally am a stickler for the truth. I

confront a problem, apply the brain no matter how badly it reflects on me personally and then act on it. My brother Rory is a sweeper under the carpet. Both attitudes have a lot to recommend them and a lot going against them. Problems can be dissected or glossed over and it is difficult to decide which is the best approach. You can find yourself going round and round in circles when sometimes it is best just to press on regardless.

12. Rehashing previous day and nights unsuccessful conversations.

The whole point of these exercises is to put you in fine fettle. Each letter of that word stands for something: F is feeling, T is thinking, T is talking, L is listening and the two Es are your ears. What you do between your ears should make you and other people feel good.

CONCLUSION

'Art is parasitic on life as criticism is parasitic on art,' said theatre critic Kenneth Tynan. D. H. Lawrence fought against this his entire life and, according to his wife, ultimately failed. 'He seemed to me to have fallen between two stools as so many writers do. He wanted to have his cake and eat it. He could not accept the narrow social world and yet he didn't believe in a wider human one. Commentators and critics of life and nothing more.'

Unlike Lawrence, I am not dismissive of the social world, but to enjoy it I need to develop my Primary Self, with its speech patterns and modes of thought. That is the point of this book, whose lessons I recommend not just to other people but also to myself. 'Always this desolating, agonised feeling that she was outside of life, an onlooker, whilst Ursula was a partaker,' writes Lawrence of the envious Hermione, Ursula's defeated rival for the heart of Birkin in *Women in Love*. This was the crux of all Lawrence's novels. How can a person actually 'be' rather than just theorise? How can a person escape his cursed self consciousness and just be part of life?

The conventional reply to that question is to busy yourself with activity of one sort or another and fill your leisure time with treats, distractions and hobbies, but Lawrence would dismiss such a strategy as ultimately doomed to failure. He believed in encounter not evasion and he must be right because everybody wakes up one day in their middle age and vainly asks themselves the point of it all.

E. M. Forster famously says the point is connection: whether it is with people, culture, nature or even God. Lawrence advocates the binning of compromise and the immersion of 'self' in the present. I say they are both right. My way to life is power through words.

187

Talk, the subject of this book, is all about connecting with other people through language, but what gives you talk power is a happy marriage between your thought and your words. That's the point of keeping a diary.

A word of caution. So much of what we do and say is calculated. Obviously, love and money are extreme situations where all you are trying to achieve is persuasion. You know how crippling it can be when you are madly in love with somebody. It's a relief when you don't see them because it is so exhausting having to impress them all the time. When you're with them, suddenly there is not a natural bone in your body and your tongue obstinately fails to wag in its usual scintillating manner, despite your every effort to appear nonchalantly charming. Of course, the golden goal in one's relations with others is mutual self liberation so that together you express your thoughts and feelings spontaneously without a care in the world or of it. That is the *craic*.

The key is not to want or need anything off anybody else – not love, friendship, connections, money, approval, recommendations, or even attention. The aim is to live in the moment of the word – but that does not mean to say you should not practice it, remember it, polish it, embellish it, perfect it and grow to love it.

POSTSCRIPT

They say the best way to learn is to teach and, though I say it myself, I have learnt a lot from having written this book – although, of course, the simple act of friendship is worth a thousand of these books. It teaches you everything you need to know about how to get on with other people.

The point of this book is to remind those amongst us what we learnt as children in the playground at school, but who in the course of our dutiful lives have lost the knack, the necessary gamesmanship to make real friends out of the multitude of contacts, acquaintances, relations and people we call friends.

Iconic guitarist Eric Clapton actually suggests fishing as 'a great way to get back to being a social human being'. Presumably it readjusts your attitude to time. It keeps you still. It occupies your Primary Self so you can inadvertently access your Second Self. It gives you silence. Hardly anything happens. You are *Waiting for Godot*. It serves no other purpose and you are desperate for conversation after a long solitary and probably cold and wet day on the river.

APPENDIX

VOCAB LISTS (*Make your own*)

Current Affairs (politics)

Nouns:

legacy	conflict	principle
predecessor	delegate	figure
opponent	ideology	decline
controversy	lobby	programme
candidate	nomination	settlement
inquiry	platform	approach
disquiet	pundit	commitment
reform	coalition	quality
hostility	turn-out	expectation
achievement	constitution	activist
record	process	response
concession	compromise	rival
circumstances	motive	issues
conception	system	practices
operator	commentator	perception
impasse	statement	initiative
opposition	stance	endorsement
conflict	position	strategy
opposition	relations	momentum

Verbs:

To devise	run	expose
rule out	secure	confront
pursue	design	launch
urge	axe	embark

Verbs continued:

attribute	propose	alienate
establish	support	address
represent	operate	concede.

Adjectives:

compromised	incumbent	facing
marked	fundamental	comparable
matched	sustainable	integral
domestic	ideological	resistant
corresponding	aspirant	defining

Culture (books and films)

Nouns:

tone	relevance	action
wit	material	familiarity
theme	attention	performance
matter	disclosure	study
diatribe	parallel	momentum
approach	insight	contrast
accuracy	scope	treatment
territory	exchange	presence
domain	summary	subject
account	view	norm
background	reservation	redemption
narrative	dimension	appeal
evocation	research	trademark
portrayal	pace	nuance
demonstration	issues	response
adjustment	motif	theme
dilemma	pace	aspect
evidence	portrait	resolution
tendency	tension	feature
fulfilment	freshness	
realisation	tendency	

Verbs:

To translate	occur	associate
examine	transform	compare
report	persist	focus
convey	punctuate	enhance
capture	scrutinised	portray
rely	give rise	deliver
suggest	overshadow	capitalise
unfold	shine	involve
depict	expect	highlight
become apparent	set in	link
shift	detract	emerge

Adjectives:

mannered	flawed	compelling
(un)convincing	complex	sensitive
intent	well drawn	dynamic
lyrical	engaging	subversive
meticulous	plausible	stylistic
embellished	authentic	symbolic
unresolved	evocative	familiar
banal	handled	adapted